Joseph Parrish Thompson

Christianity and Emancipation

Or the Teachings and the Influence of the Bible Against Slavery

Joseph Parrish Thompson

Christianity and Emancipation
Or the Teachings and the Influence of the Bible Against Slavery

ISBN/EAN: 9783744730488

Printed in Europe, USA, Canada, Australia, Japan

Cover: Foto ©Lupo / pixelio.de

More available books at **www.hansebooks.com**

CHRISTIANITY AND EMANCIPATION;

OR,

THE TEACHINGS AND THE INFLUENCE

OF THE

BIBLE AGAINST SLAVERY.

BY

JOSEPH P. THOMPSON,

PASTOR OF THE BROADWAY TABERNACLE CHURCH.

NEW YORK:
ANSON D. F. RANDOLPH,
No. 683 BROADWAY.
1863.

EDWARD O. JENKINS,
Printer & Stereotyper,
No. 20 North William St.

NEW YORK, May 1st, 1863.

REV. JOS. P. THOMPSON, D. D.,

DEAR SIR,—Having listened with much interest to your sermon on the influence of the Christian religion on the abolition of slavery, and regarding the views you then presented as of vital importance to the church and nation at the present time, we request a copy of the discourse for publication, and remain

Your friends,

SETH B. HUNT,	CHARLES ABERNETHY,
WM. HENRY SMITH,	L. M. BATES,
WM. G. LAMBERT,	SAMUEL HOLMES,
ADON SMITH,	CHAS. S. SMITH.

NEW YORK, May 4th, 1863.

GENTLEMEN,—I thank you for your friendly expressions concerning my Fast-Day Sermon. If its argument, the result of years of patient study, will at all contribute to elucidate the teaching, and vindicate the honor, of the sacred Scriptures in respect to the system of slavery, it is quite at your disposal.

With high regard,

Yours truly,

JOS. P. THOMPSON.

MESSRS. SETH B. HUNT,
WM. H. SMITH, and others.

(3)

CHRISTIANITY AND EMANCIPATION.

I.

A SLANDER UPON THE GOSPEL.

A MONSTROUS libel upon Christianity has lately appeared from the pen of the Professor of History in the University of Ghent. It is the most shocking scandal that the Deism of this age, or of any age, has invented against the Bible. There is nothing more malignant in Voltaire; and, though it is couched in decent phrase, there is scarce anything more blasphemous in Thomas Paine. It is contained in half-a-dozen lines, imbedded in a work of several octavo volumes, entitled, "Studies upon the History of Humanity;" and may be found in the chapter on the enfranchisement of serfs, in the volume upon "Feudalism and the Church."* Shall I then reproduce it in the English tongue, and give it currency in a nation that its author could not reach? Alas, it is already current wherever modern Deism assails the divine origin of the Bible; it has found utterance in lyceums and conventions, in newspapers and magazines, as the favorite, because the most effective, weapon of modern infidelity. And yet I shudder to write these impious

---

* *La Féodalité et L'Eglise*, par F. Laurent. *Etudes sur L'Histoire de L'Humanité* Tome VII., pp. 595 and 613. Paris, E. Jung-Treuttel.

words :—"To have done anything," says Laurent, "toward the enfranchisement of the servile classes, the Church had need of a living sentiment of liberty. But Christianity never had that sentiment: it accepted slavery by consecrating it with its authority. Yes, Christianity did more than accept slavery; it saw in it a Divine institution. It is not enough to say that Christianity does not condemn slavery; it would be more true to say that it sanctifies it."*

This horrible calumny against Christianity is used by its author to glorify the French Revolution of 1789, as an intervention of God in behalf of humanity, to inaugurate liberty and equality in spite of the church. Theodore Parker charged upon the Bible the same infamous complicity with slavery, and sneered at the idea of a supernatural revelation in the Scriptures.† Such a Bible was to him a Fetish. "The divine statutes in the

---

* The same sentiment is expressed by Patrice Larroque, in his treatise "*de l'Esclavage chez les Nations Chrétiennes*," p. 13. "Not only have the books of the New Testament not one solitary text against slavery, but all that they say about slavery is favorable to its principle. And it must not be forgotten, that Christianity, starting from the books of the Old Testament, declares those to have been revealed and inspired by the Holy Spirit, as well as the books of the New Testament. But slavery finds its justification in express utterances of the Old Testament."

† Theodore Parker's "Experience as a Minister," pp. 64 and 143. Mr. Parker takes these sentiments to represent the current views of "Bible-worshippers," as he designates believers in the inspiration of the Scriptures. He does not, however, deny or disprove the interpretation of the Bible which he imputes to such persons; but assuming that the Old Testament does sanction slavery, he makes this a reason for rejecting its divine inspiration. Bishop Colenso reasons in the same way against the inspiration of the Pentateuch. He first misinterprets the Hebrew text, and having charged upon it the most extravagant errors and immoralities, he then refuses to believe that his *imaginary* Bible comes from God—a conclusion in which we quite agree.

Old Testament admitted the principle that man might own a man as well as a garden or an ox. Moses and the prophets were on the side of slavery ; and neither Paul of Tarsus nor Jesus of Nazareth uttered a direct word against it, ... the slaveholder finds the chief argument for his ownership of men, in texts from the authentic Word of God." Mr. Parker had the popular reputation of kr ing many languages : he ought to have known Hebrew better than to have conceded that the Old Testament sanctions or in any sense admits the ownership of man in man. But the Deist who charges the Bible with sanctioning slavery, knows well that this is the most odious and damaging accusation that he could bring against a book claiming to have come from God ; that in an enlightened age,—an age when moral convictions and philanthropic sympathies have combined to exterminate slavery as a sin and a curse—nothing could more effectually destroy all respect for the Bible, or disprove its divine origin, than the representation that it sanctions the owning of human beings. This imputation is "a blow aimed at all that good men hold most sacred. It seeks to undermine the very foundations of national morality and break the spring of all public and private virtue. It attacks Christianity in its central principle and vital essence. It daringly assaults the morality of the Bible, and seeks to destroy forever its authority by making it an accomplice in the perpetuation of the most gigantic crimes."*

* London Daily News.

II.

SLAVERY IN THE TIME OF CHRIST.

TEST this charge of complicity with slavery by your own moral sense. When Christ appeared, slavery was universal in the Roman empire. What the system was, we know from its laws that have come down to us, and from glimpses of Roman life and manners in the classic writers. The Romans perfected the system of legalized chattelism. Their laws reduced the slave to the level of cattle. "Slaves were held *pro nullis, pro mortuis, pro quadrupedibus.* They were not entitled to the rights and considerations of matrimony. They could be sold, transferred, pawned as goods or personal estate, for goods they were, and as such they were esteemed. They might be tortured for evidence, punished at the discretion of their lord, and even put to death by his authority.*" Scourges loaded with lead, or furnished with prongs, the yoke, the brand, the pincers, the rack, were common instruments of torture ; and there were torturers by profession, to whom masters sometimes sent their slaves for the refinements of cruelty. Many a trifling offence was punished by crucifixion. Augustus ordered his steward to be crucified on the mast of his ship for having killed and eaten a game quail prized by the emperor.† Field hands were commonly purchased

---

* Taylor on Civil Law, in Cooper's *Justinian*, p. 411.
† Bib. Repository, Vol. VI., pp. 422, 423. Also, Plutarch Apophth. VI., 778.

in the slave market, at an age capable of labor ; and
"when through age or infirmity they had become in-
capable of working, they were again sent with other
refuse to the market. They were often chained to their
work in the field ; and an underground cellar, for the
imprisonment of slaves by night, was a necessary part
of the farm buildings on a large plantation. The whole
system was pervaded by the unscrupulous spirit charac-
teristic of the power of capital. Slaves and cattle were
placed on the same level. The slave and the ox were
fed properly so long as they could work, because it
would not have been good economy to let them starve ;
and they were sold like a worn-out plough-share when
they became unable to work, because it would not have
been good economy to maintain them longer."*

* Mommsen's History of Rome, Vol. II., p. 368.   Prof. Döllinger, of Munich, a
scholar of wide research, says, "The slave in Rome was a chattel and a possession, had no individuality or 'caput;' whatever he earned belonged to his master,
and he might be made a present of, lent, pawned, or exchanged.   His union with
a wife was no marriage, that is, was devoid of all its privileges and effects, and
only a contubernium or cohabitation.   A master might torture or kill his slave at
will ; there was no one to prevent his doing so, or to bring him to account.   The
modes of torture and punishment were various and cruel, and the ordinary punishment of death was crucifixion.   One cruel infliction frequently resorted to for
female slaves was chaining to a block of wood, which served the poor sufferer for
a seat, and which she had to drag about with her day and night.   Slaves in the
country, who had to till the ground, were chained by the foot, and kept at night
in an ergastulum, or underground room.   The Roman law inflicted the punishment
of death for killing a plough-ox, while the murderer of a slave was called to no
account whatever.
   "It is in vain one looks for anything like common human feeling in the Roman
slave-law of republican times, and that of the earlier empire.   The breaking up of
slave families was entirely in the hands of the merchant or the owner ; husband
might be separated from wife, and mother from children, all dispersed and sold off
into the houses of strangers and to foreign towns.   Slavery is equivalent to death
in the eye of the civil law, which does not admit the existence of a slave ; which

This was the rule of even the best masters. We have it on the authority of Plutarch, that the elder Cato, the great economist of Rome, who sought to restrain the luxury of the nation, and to inspire its patriotism,—this type of Roman virtue, taught, that as soon as slaves grew too old to do their tale of work, they should be sold off or otherwise disposed of, so as not to be a burden to the master. Having taken the work out of his servants as out of brute beasts, he turned them off in their old age.*

Such was the cruel system of slavery, and such its inhuman practices, as established by usage and sustained by law throughout the Roman empire, when Christ appeared. Do you believe that his teachings, or those of his apostles, sanctioned this system of human chattelism? Where do you find that sanction? Is it in Christ's announcement of his mission—"I am come to preach the Gospel to the poor; to preach deliverance to the captives; to set at liberty them that are bruised; to preach the acceptable year [the Jubilee] of the Lord?" Do you find the sanction of slavery in Christ's exposition of the law—"Thou shalt love thy neighbor as thyself?" Do you find it in his own heavenly rule of life—"Whatsoever ye would that men should to you, do ye even so to them?"

---

entirely avoids and annuls the contract of a master with his slave; gives the slave no action at law against him; admits not of adultery being committed by or with one of them, and compels female slaves to surrender themselves to their master's lust against their will." "The Gentile and the Jew," Vol. II., pp. 259-264.

* Plutarch, Life of Cato Major.

"I defy the most unfeeling planter to go, immediately after hearing these words, to the slave-market to buy slaves ; and I defy the most resolute critic to maintain, after having read them, that the gospel does not condemn slavery."*

Do you then find the sanction of slavery in Paul's instructions to masters and servants, given in view of slavery as an existing state of society? Do you find anything that can be tortured into an approval of this system in the command—"Masters, give unto your servants that which is just and equal ; knowing that ye also have a master in heaven ; neither is there respect of persons with him."† Do you find your gospel warrant for slavery in the warning of James to the rich and proud oppressors of that age—"Behold, the hire of the laborers who have reaped down your fields, which is of you kept back by fraud, crieth ; and the cries of them which have reaped, are entered into the ears of the Lord of Sabaoth ?"‡

Aristotle, in his ethics, had attempted to establish slavery upon a philosophical principle, as an institution founded by nature in the distinctions of races and in the conditions necessary to human society. Against the opinion that the division of mankind into freemen and slaves is created by the law of force, and is therefore unjust, he argues, that some men are born as far inferior to others as the brute nature is below the

* *Cochin*, Results of slavery ; Miss Booth's translation, p. 311.
† Coloss. iv. 1., and Ephes. vi. 9.   ‡ James v. 4.

human, and that such persons were designed by nature
to be "the animated instruments" of the household and
of society in procuring the necessaries and performing
the labors of life. And since these instruments are
not only necessary for procuring property, but are
themselves a kind of property, he defines a slave to
be "one who by the law of nature does not belong to
himself, but who, though a man, belongs to another.
He is *the man of another man*."*   •

Place this argument of the great publicist and ethical
philosopher of Stagira, in favor of slavery, by the side
of the teachings of Paul to masters and servants, and
determine whether Paul so much as allows that man-
owning which Aristotle justifies and approves from
the law of nature. Place the system of slavery itself
as it existed in the Roman empire, side by side with
the gospel of Christ, and answer to your own candid
judgment, Do you believe that the gospel sanctions slavery? And then let your moral sense answer this further
question :—If the gospel did approve this system
of man-owning, could you believe that the gospel came
from God? When the nature of slavery is fairly understood, can infidelity devise a more telling and sneering
accusation against the Bible than this—that it sanctions
slavery, and sanctifies it as a divine institution?

---

* See Aristotle's Polit. and his Nic. Ethics. Also, the admirable summary in
Döllinger II., 227, and in Paul Janet, Histoire de la Philosophie Morale, I., 193.

III.

THE QUESTION STATED.

To rebut this monstrous calumny upon the Bible, we have simply to examine the Bible itself, and to trace its influence upon the institution of slavery. But, before going into this examination, we must settle the meaning of terms, that there may be no evasion with regard to the result. What, then, is SLAVERY? When this question is asked of an American audience, it can refer to but one thing—the system of slavery as established by law in the Southern States. It is not some abstract relation of master and servant, concerning which we inquire, it is not some antiquated condition of society that we are seeking to explore, it is not some speculative theory of the relations of capital and labor ;—it is the actual, concrete, definitive system before our eyes in the South ; and that which concerns us is not a usage without law, nor the abuses of a social system, nor the character of individual slaveholders—but the condition of slavery as defined by law. Now, the essential fact in slavery is not the authority of the master over the servant, nor the dependence of the servant upon the master, nor the behavior of the individual master toward his servant, nor the physical condition and treatment of the slave, but the *ownership* of the slave vested in the master by law.

This ownership of a human being, as an article of property, is the essential feature of American slavery. In this respect it exactly copies the Roman slavery of the time of the apostles. By judicial decisions under Southern law, "slaves are deemed, held, taken, reputed and adjudged in law to be chattels personal in the hands of their owners and possessors, and their executors, administrators, and assigns, to all intents, constructions and purposes whatsoever."* That is the *legal* condition of the slave : and that condition. of a human being declared by law a chattel, an article of property or merchandise, defines the essential nature of slavery. The privation of every right, the possibility of every wrong, is couched in this one principle of Southern law, that the slave is a chattel.

Keeping this in mind, I ask again, Does CHRISTIANITY SANCTION SLAVERY ? But we must also define Christianity. The Ghent professor, with the very art of Voltaire, confounds Christianity with the Roman Catholic Church, and thus charges upon the gospel the hostility to liberty which he alleges against that church. But Christianity is not to be identified with any ecclesiastical system, nor with the opinions and practices of any of its ministers or professors. It has its own text-book,

---

* South Carolina code, Prince's Digest, 446. The Louisiana civil code, Art. 35, declares that " a slave is one who is in the power of a master to whom he belongs. The master may sell him, dispose of his person, his industry, and his labor. He can do nothing, possess nothing, nor acquire anything, but what must belong to his master." This principle has been abundantly maintained by Southern courts. (See in Wheeler's Law of Slavery, Stroud's Sketch of the Laws relating to Slavery, Goodell's American Slave Code, etc.)

and its spirit and teachings must be learned directly
from the New Testament.

Thus placing Slavery and Christianity side by side, I
affirm, that neither in the New Testament nor in the
Old, neither by precept nor by example, neither by pre-
cedent nor by indirection, does the Bible sanction slavery ; but that the religion of the Bible is thoroughly
hostile to slavery, in spirit and in principle, in precept
and in practice.

The evidence upon this point is both critical and historical. The critical inquiry must embrace an analysis
of the Mosaic laws of servitude, and the attitude of
Christianity toward slavery, in the teachings of Christ
and his apostles, or in the Apostolic age. The historical inquiry, starting from the age of the New Testament, will, for convenience, trace the influence of Christianity upon slavery :

(1.) From the time of the Apostles to the time of
Constantine ;—when the new religion, struggling for its
own life, first came into contact with the organized
iniquities of the pagan world.

(2.) Its influence upon slavery from Constantine till
the Reformation ; and,

(3.) The relations of the gospel to slavery in modern
Christendom.

IV.

THE TEACHINGS OF CHRIST.

WHAT was the attitude of Christianity toward slavery in the apostolic age? For the answer, we go directly to the New Testament. When our Lord began his ministry, whatever kind of bond-service had formerly existed among the Jews, servitude had ceased to be an institution of Hebrew society. There was' then no such thing as a system of slavery in Judea. Here and there, a Roman officer appears to have had a few house or body slaves. Herod, the Idumean, had such servants. Possibly some of the wealthier Jews, also, had servants over whom they claimed the right of control. " But in the time of the second temple, we know that no slaves were held by the Essenes, or by the Therapeutæ; for these sects rejected all slavery, as in contravention with the natural equality of men. The Pharisees, too, were, on moral grounds, opposed to the holding of many slaves, and recommended instead, for household service, the employment of indigent Hebrews."* In the time of Christ, the Jews, to whom our Lord addressed his personal ministry, were not, in any proper sense, a slave-holding people; and though there were occasional traces of the old Mosaic code of servitude, this was fast

---

* *Mielziner*, translated in Am. Theol. Review, Vol. III., p 426. See also p. 52 of the original, *Die Verhält nisse der sklaven bei den alten Hebräern.*

dying out under the combined influence of Roman sub-
jugation and domestic poverty; so that there was nothing in the immediate sphere of Christ's labors to call
forth a discussion upon the specific evil of slavery.
No such case appears in the gospel history.*

But the principles laid down by Christ in his discourse at Nazareth, and in the sermon on the mount,
are conclusive against the claim of property in man.
No man would dream of framing a slave-code out of
the words of Christ; of buying or selling a human being by a warrant from the lips of Jesus, or of quoting
anything that Christ said as a justification of slavery.
Had Jesus of Nazareth excepted the seed of Ham, or
the negro, or any class or race, from his proclamation
of grace and deliverance, he could not have commanded
our homage as the Redeemer of mankind. Every slaveholder knows that an honest application of Christ's
golden rule would compel him to relinquish all pretense
to property in his fellow-man. Not the most profane
audacity of the advocates of slavery, nor the most malignant ingenuity of infidels, has ever attempted to fasten
upon Christ himself the sanctioning of slavery by word
or deed. The utmost that has been alleged on this
point is that he uttered nothing directly against it.
Neither did Christ say anything against the tyrannous
family laws of the Romans, or the brutal gladiatorial
shows. But there is strong presumptive evidence that

* See the author's "Teachings of the New Testament on Slavery" (1856), pp.
15 and 50.

in the limited sphere of his ministry, slavery did not come before him for judgment either in fact or in theory; and he did lay down principles that make it impossible for a man to hold his fellow as a slave. Would slaveholders consent to have their claims determined by the teachings of Christ, or to put these into the hands of slaves as a manual of their duties?

The apostles, especially Paul, in going forth from Judea to propagate Christianity, came in contact with Roman slavery as I have just described it; and the apostolic letters contain several allusions to this system. As Jews versed in the old Testament, the apostles were familiar with the laws of Moses in regard to master and servant. Now, the recognition of slavery, in the sense that our usage and Southern laws attach to the word, cannot be found in the institutes of Moses.

V.

SERVITUDE AMONG THE HEBREWS.

In discussing the nature of Hebrew servitude, it is unnecessary to go back of the time of Moses. Abraham, like the Arab sheikh of to-day, had around him a body, not of chattel slaves, but of household retainers, owing fealty to their lord; men whom he trusted with the stewardship of all his property; whom he armed for the rescue of Lot, and led into battle; to one of whom he committed the delicate office of seeking a bride for

Isaac, sending him with a tempting dowry into a distant land.

As to the "seed of Ham," our Sabbath schools have made this generation sufficiently familiar with the Bible to know that Noah's curse was definitively pronounced upon Canaan, Ham's youngest son, and was accomplished when the Israelites subdued the Canaanites. But if any still insist upon applying it perpetually to the whole posterity of Ham, I must remind them that the grand old empires of Egypt, Chaldea, and Assyria, were all founded by immediate descendants of Ham, and that these Hamitic nations successively enslaved the Israelites, the posterity of Shem. I must remind such, also, that the descent of the negro race from Ham has never been satisfactorily established, upon grounds either of physiology, of history, or of philology. Indeed, the evidence rather preponderates in the opposite scale. Moreover, Aben Ezra and Mendelssohn, two of the greatest names in Hebrew philology, maintain that the expression "servant of servants" in Genesis ix. 25, does not describe the *abjectness* of the condition, but simply the *relative* condition in the family, whether of the individual or of nations. The Hebrew idiom is literally *servant, servants*, which, according to these philologers, merely designates the class without stigmatizing or aggravating the condition: "He shall be [not the slave of slaves, but] a servant—belonging to the class of servants." The learned authors of the Septuagint version point the verse differently, and come at the same meaning: "Cursed be Canaan the servant ($\pi\alpha\tilde{\imath}\varsigma$); a house-servant ($o\iota\kappa\acute{\epsilon}\tau\eta\varsigma$) shall he be to his brethren":— i. e., he shall be in a menial condition.

Some would interpret this prophetic imprecation by the relative position of the Hamitic, the Japhetic, and the Shemitic nations, in the march of civilization. "To the nations of the race of Ham was accorded an inferior and subservient position in the great programme of the world's progress: that of pioneers subserving the material wealth and secular advancement of mankind."* There is a general historic truth in this view, and yet Rawlinson justly assigns to the earlier Hamitic nations a higher role in the world's drama. "Egypt and Babylon—Mizraim and Nimrod—both descendants of Ham—led the way, and acted as the pioneers of mankind in the various untrodden fields of art, literature, and science. Alphabetic writing, astronomy, history, chronology, architecture, plastic art, sculpture, navigation, agriculture, textile industry, seem, all of them, to have had their origin in one or other of these two countries."†

This author furnishes many cogent arguments for the Hamitic origin of the primitive people of Babylon, which, indeed, is distinctly asserted in Genesis x. 8. But he gives special prominence to the discovery, in the most ancient remains of Chaldea, of a form of speech older than the known Babylonian language, "whose vocabulary is

---

* Dr. Leonard Bacon, New Englander, 1862, pp. 853, 354.
† History of the Five Great Monarchies, I., p. 75.

decidedly Cushite, or Ethiopian." The seed of Ham were the progenitors of the mightiest empires of the old world.* The great orientalist of the, College of France takes a middle ground between these two views of the relation of the Hamitic nations to human progress. According to Ernest Renan, the Chinese in eastern Asia, the Cushites and Hamites, in western Asia, and in Africa, were the earliest civilized races ; but their civilization was stamped with a materialistic character—the religious and poetic instincts but little developed, with little artistic feeling, but a great aptitude for the manual arts, and for the exact and practical sciences. These Cushite and Hamitic civilizations disappeared before the advance of the Shemitic and the Arian types, which, though at first greatly inferior to the former in external civilization, in material works, and in the science of organization which makes great empires, yet infinitely surpassed them in vigor, courage, and the genius of poetry and religion. Yet Renan concedes to the Hamitic nations, for a long period, "the monopoly of commerce, navigation, and industrial arts."†

In a word, then, the curse of Noah was not pronounced upon "the seed of Ham," but only upon Canaan ; or if intended for "the seed of Ham," it was not in any sense, and never has proved to be in fact, a curse of personal slavery. It cannot, with logical or historical fairness, be applied to the existing negro races.

* History of the Five Great Monarchies, I., pp. 64, 65.
† *Histoire Générale et Système Comparé des Langues Sémitiques.* Vol. I, pp. 500–503. Third edition, Paris, 1863.

VI.

THE STATUTES OF MOSES IN REGARD TO SERVANTS.

EVERY competent scholar, be he Jew or Christian, knows that the idea of property in man, of a human chattel, is entirely unknown to the Mosaic code. Among the Jews, a price was sometimes paid in advance for the use and control of a servant, and such a servant was said to be "bought with money;" and so, too, money was paid to the father in consideration of the hand of a daughter.* Yet neither wife or servant thus "bought with money," became the legal property of the possessor, but the servant, as well as the wife, was a *person* still, with rights guarded by religion and by law. Among the Hebrews, involuntary servitude, whether a penalty for debt or a misfortune of war, had nothing in common with the *chattelism* of more recent times. Under the Mosaic code, the relation of master and servant was so hedged round by laws in the interest of the servant, and was so often broken up by the periodical manumission of the bondman, that chattel slavery, or

---

* This custom prevails among eastern nations at this day. Dr. Perkins states that "wives are purchased among the Nestorians, as they were in the days of Jacob—the price ranging from five to fifty or one hundred dollars, according to the standing and charms of the person. It is not considered proper for the father of the bride, who receives the purchase money, to appropriate it to his private purposes, but to expend it in furnishing her with wedding garments. —*Residence in Persia*, p. 236.

the permanent and unmitigated ownership of man in man, was clearly impossible.

The ablest writers upon the Hebrew economy, such as the learned Jew, *Dr. Mielziner*, of Copenhagen, *Heinrich Ewald*, of Göttingen, a great authority in Hebrew antiquities, Prof. *Joseph L. Saalschütz*, of Königsberg, whose works on the Mosaic polity are of the highest standing, *Joseph Salvador*, the Rabbinical scholar of Paris—men versed in the Hebrew language and in Jewish customs—agree in this : that the laws of Moses nowhere recognize the right of property in man, nor concede to the master an absolute proprietorship over the person of his servant.

The term generally used in the Mosaic code to designate one in a servile condition, was "a common name for all who stood in a dependent or subordinate relation. It had not the degrading sense which we connect with the words *slave* or *bondman ;* but it often had the mild significancy which we associate, in certain relations, with the word *servant.*"* Nor was there any other term in use among the Hebrews which would correspond with our use of the term slave, to denote one held in the possession of another as his property. "The Mosaic law knows nothing of *slavery* in the sense of considering *freeman* and *slave* as beings holding an opposite relation to each other in respect to their dignity as men, and on a scale of civil and social rights. The Hebrew language has no word for stigmatizing by a degrading appellation

* Mielziner, Die Verhältnisse, p. 11; or Am. Theo. Review, Vol. III., p. 231. The term here referred to (*Ebed*) is derived from a verb which signifies to *labor ;* *i. g.,* "six days mayst thou labor ;" or to *serve ; e. g., servants* of the king.

one part of those who owe service, and distinguishing
them from the rest as 'slaves,' but only *one* term for all
who are under obligation to render service to others.
For males, this is *Ebed, servant, man-servant;* properly,
laborer; for females, *Shifchah, Ama, maid-servant,
maid.* Among a people who occupied themselves with
agriculture ; whose lawgiver, Moses, and whose kings,
Saul and David, went immediately from the herd and
from the plough to their high vocation, there could be
nothing degrading in an appellation taken from 'labor.'
The laws respecting servants protect in every regard
their dignity and their feelings as men. They by no
means surrendered these to the arbitrary will of the masters, as in other ancient and modern states in which
slavery and thralldom have prevailed."*

The terms buying and selling, applied to one form of
contract under which Hebrew servants were procured,†
mislead the reader of the English Bible, who associates
with these words the idea of the transfer of an article of
property for a consideration in money. But the Hebrew
term for this " buying " is as indeterminate as the word
for " servant." It strictly means to *get* for one's self, to
gain, to *acquire*, to *obtain*, without reference either to

* Saalschütz, *Das Mosaiche Recht*, Kap. 101: " *Dienende.*" See also in Bib.
Sacra, Vol. XIX., p. 33.

† Ex. xxi. 2. "If thou *buy* a Hebrew servant." The learned Jewish doctor, M.
Kalisch, of London, translates this, " When thou *acquirest* a servant;" and he adds,
" there exists in Hebrew no word for *slave* in the sense of an individual who is con
sidered merely as an instrument: the Hebrew word means merely *laborer*, and the
most privileged favorites of God are called ' *servants* of God.'"—*Commentary on
Exodus.*

the mode of procuring or to the nature of the tenure.* Eve uses it at the birth of Cain : "I have *gotten* a man from the Lord." (Gen. iv. 11.) It is applied to *getting* wisdom and understanding. (Prov. iv. 7 ; xv. 32 ; xvi. 16 ; xix. 8.) The Lord *purchased* his people (Ex. xv. 16), and Mount Zion (Ps. lxxviii. 54). "Is not He [the Lord] thy father that hath *bought* thee ?" (Deut. xxxii. 6.) Boaz *purchased* Ruth to be his wife. (Ruth iv. 10.) But did the heroine of that charming Hebrew pastoral, the direct ancestress of David and of our Lord, become the *property* of that "mighty man of wealth" who paid court to her innocent beauty by the magnificence of his dowry, paid in presence of the elders and of all the people? Did Boaz "buy" Ruth in the sense in which a Southern planter buys a quadroon?

Hence, wherever the Hebrew Scriptures apply this indeterminate word "buying" to denote the acquisition of a person, whether as wife or as servant, the vital question is, "*into what relation* the so-called act of purchase brings the person purchased."† Thus, according to Exodus xxi. 8, a man could "*sell* his daughter to be a maid-servant ;" and, according to Leviticus xxv. 39, a man could sell himself and his family for debt ; but the context shows that the so-called sale did not make the subject of it a chattel in the hands of the purchaser ; for in the one case the maiden was "betrothed," and had the

* *Genesius,* art. קָנָה *kan-nah.*

† Prof. Barrowes, in Bib. Sac., Vol. XIX., p. 565.

connubial rights of a consort of second rank ;* and in
the other, the debtor merely mortgaged his labor for a
term of years.† Where the servant is spoken of as his
master's "money" (Exodus xxi. 20, 21), the sense is ob-
viously, not that he was an article of property, but that,
on account of his services, he was worth money to his
master.‡ The presumption of the law was that no master would wantonly injure a servant who was valuable to
himself ; yet if, in a passion, the master killed a servant,
the law would call him to account, not for the destruction
of his own "property," but for the death of a man.§   In
a word, under the Mosaic law, the servant, however acquired, and by whatever tenure held, was always a *person*, never a *chattel*.

To understand the law of Hebrew servitude, we must
keep in mind the system of property and of labor among
the Jews, and also their penal code. The agrarian dis-
tribution of land after the conquest of Palestine made
every Jewish householder a landowner as well ; and the
homestead could not be alienated for a longer period than
the year of the coming Jubilee.‖ Thus agriculture was
made the basis of the State, with a subdivision of its territory as minute as now obtains in parts of France. With

---

* Kalisch.   *Com. in loc.*

† A similar usage of mortgaging the debtor to the creditor obtains in the Indian
Archipelago. It is there called by the Dutch, *Pandelingschap, bond-debtorship*
See note to p. 27.

‡ See in *Bib. Sacra*, XIX., p. 583 ; *New Englander*, XVIII., p. 361.

§ By the Rabbinical interpretation, the master was executed by the sword. See
Philippson, *Der Pentateuch*, Commentary on Ex. xx.

‖ *Jahn*, Heb. Archæology, § 55.

this broad basis of equal prosperity, while the Hebrew code enjoins personal kindness to the poor, it does not legalize pauperism ; it has neither "poor-rates" nor "alms-houses." "The Mosaic law knows nothing of *mendicants*, properly so called ; and even the word mendicant is not found in the Old Testament."* Nor does it provide houses of detention and correction for vagrants, or prisons for thieves and debtors. Though imprisonment was common in Egypt and in other nations of antiquity, and though it was introduced as a punishment among the Jews in the time of their kings, there is no trace of this method of punishment in the Mosaic code, except, perhaps, the detention of a criminal for trial (Lev. xxiv. 12);† and it is altogether probable that, for several generations, the agricultural community distributed in the small villages of Palestine had neither alms-houses nor prisons. The remedy for theft, vagrancy, or insolvency, was servitude, either voluntary or compulsory.‡

* *Munk*, Palestine, p. 212.

† *Munk*, p. 216 ; see also I. Kings xxii. 27 ; Jer. xxxii. 2.

‡ Maimonides enumerates four degrees of punishment: *Death, excision, scourging,* and *admonition.* (Reasons for the Laws of Moses, Chap. XVI.) *Munk* adds fining, or the *amende.* (Palestine, p. 215.) But the code also provides that in certain circumstances the thief " shall be sold for his theft." (Exodus xxii. 3.) A somewhat similar code exists among the natives of the Indian Archipelago. In a state of society where personal property is small, and real estate is unknown ; where there is no such thing as hired labor for wages ; where there are no prisons, and the only punishments are bodily chastisement and death, there exists a custom which consigns the idle pauper and the insolvent debtor to a condition between the citizen and the slave. The Dutch residents of Sumatra call such a person a *Pandeling*—a bond-debtman, one held as a pledge. The person of the debtor, or of one of his nearest kin, is placed under the control of the creditor, who supports him, but exacts from his labor the payment of the debt, or, at least, of the interest. The debtor can change masters if he can find any one to buy up the claim. This peculiar institu-

Among a primitive agricultural people, occupying a small and subdivided territory, surrounded by jealous and hostile neighbors, when the customs of war gave the captive but the alternative of slavery or death ; and in an age when society had not yet risen to those two great measures of thrift and safety—systematic wages for labor, and legalized imprisonment for robbery and theft—involuntary servitude was a temporary expedient for disposing alike of captives, and of debtors and criminals. And so far forth—that is, as a provisional penal code, as a police regulation, or as a temporary military or economical necessity—such servitude was allowed in the Jewish commonwealth. The term "domiciliary imprisonment" has been happily applied by Cochin to describe this feature of the Hebrew police ;—a system which finds a parallel in the domestication of Indian servants, in the early history of New England. Thus, by the laws of Plymouth colony, vagrant Indian children could be bound to service by the selectmen ; and Indian debtors or thieves could be sold for service to satisfy the claim.

Now these penal and domiciliary regulations of Moses, so far from instituting slavery or sanctioning it as a divine constitution of human society, so limited the dura-

tion, originally equitable in principle, by degrees had degenerated into the systematic oppression of the poor and the unfortunate; and the Dutch government in the East Indies has sought to do away with the abuses of *Pandelingschap*, by bringing this arbitrary social custom under the regulation of law. The mild servitude permitted under like circumstances by the Mosaic code degenerated into the slavery recognized by the Talmud. But the Mosaic code must be judged by the social condition of the Jews at the period of its promulgation. (For an interesting sketch of *Pandelingschap*, see " *La Question de L'Esclavage, aux Etats-Unis par un ancien Fonctionnaire des Indes Néerlandaises.*" Published at the Hague, by M. Nijhoff.)

tion and conditions of even this mild servitude, as to make chattel-slavery impossible. Governmental servitude, imposing upon labor certain obligations and restraints, or subjecting vagrancy and crime to "hard labor" under a private citizen as overseer, is quite another thing from commercial slavery, which converts a man into an article of merchandise, and gives to a private individual irresponsible power over the time, the labor, and the person of another. How thoroughly the Mosaic code was opposed to this is shown in these three cardinal provisions :

1. *"He that stealeth a man and selleth him, or if he be found in his hand, he shall surely be put to death."* (Ex. xxi. 16.) The laws of Moses declare that act which is the very origin and life of African and American slavery, to be an act of piracy against human nature, to be punished with death. The learned Jew, Philo, a contemporary of Paul, thus comments upon this law, as understood by the Jews of that age :—"The kidnapper also is a thief ; and, moreover, a thief who steals the most precious treasure on earth. Therefore every one who has any regard for virtue is filled with an intense and implacable hatred of kidnappers—who, for the sake of their accursed gains, dare to impose the yoke of slavery upon those who by birth, by reason, and by nature, are their equals."* And Paul, trained a Jew, says expressly that the law was made "for the ungodly and for sinners, for unholy and profane, for murderers of

* Philo Judæus, on Special Laws.

fathers and murderers of mothers, for manslayers, for
whoremongers, for them that defile themselves with
mankind, for MEN-STEALERS, for liars, for perjured persons."

2. *"Thou shalt neither vex a stranger nor oppress him
—for ye were strangers in the land of Egypt."* (Ex.
xxii. 21.) In regard to this precept, Dr. Ludwig Philippson justly remarks, that " the deliverance of Israel
from Egypt was the foundation of their national character and constitution. The annihilation of slavery among
themselves was therefore a prime condition of their existence ; they must be a free people—a nation of the
Free."* Hence the Israelite was forbidden to retaliate
upon the children of Egyptians the oppressions of their
fathers ;† but was reminded of his own oppression in
Egypt as a motive for the kind treatment of strangers of
whatever race or nation. The same argument applies
emphatically to a people whose own national independence is based upon the declaration of man's inalienable
right to life, liberty, and the pursuit of happiness.

3. *"Thou shalt not deliver unto his master the servant
which is escaped from his master unto thee; he shall
dwell with thee, even among you in that place which he
shall choose in one of thy gates where it liketh him best ;
thou shalt not oppress him."* (Deut. xxiii. 15, 16.) Of
this precept, Maimonides, the renowned Rabbi of the
12th century, observes, that " beside the act of mercy,
it has this further beneficial result—that it teaches us to

* Der Pentateuch, *in loc.*   † Deut. xxiii. 7.

accustom ourselves to virtuous and praiseworthy actions, not only by succoring those who have sought our aid and protection, and not delivering them into the hands of those from whom they have fled, but also by promoting their comfort, doing them all manner of kindness, and not injuring or grieving them even in word."* Compare this humane provision of the Mosaic code with the *Lex Fabia* of Rome, which made it a penal offence to harbor a fugitive slave!

A code which made kidnapping and man-stealing a crime to be punished with death, which forbade the oppression of the poor and the stranger, and the returning of the fugitive slave to his master, could never have been made the foundation of that system of servitude which existed in Rome and now exists in the Southern States. The enactment of those three provisions of Hebrew law would abrogate every slave code in the South. By the Mosaic code, "the servant could have recourse to the law for all wrongs ; his testimony was received ; he could hold property and redeem himself ; he was instructed ; his rights were respected. No slave-trade, no fugitive slave law, no enslaving of natives ; a year of jubilee ; the purity of woman, the weakness of childhood, the rights of manhood placed under the provident protection of the law ; equality professed, fraternity preached. *Such* was Hebrew servitude. Let the partisans of modern slavery cease to seek arguments from it ; let them rather pattern after it !"*

---

* Reasons of the Laws of Moses, Chap. XIV.   * *Cochin*, p. 299.

Salvador declines to use even the word servitude to describe the condition of servants under the Hebrew code. The title of his chapter on this subject is, " *Dô-mesticité*, or the condition of servants improperly called slaves." He shows, conclusively, that both in theory and in practice, the Mosaic law destroyed slavery as far as this was within its power. It is a significant fact that while the history of antiquity, in Sparta, Rome, Crete, Thessaly, records frequent slave insurrections, and vigorous measures to suppress them,—in all the long history of Israel* there is no such thing as a rising of slaves, nor any legislation to prevent such insurrection;—and this for the obvious reason, that there was no such servile class in Israel as existed in other nations.

Says the Rabbi Mielziner, "No religion and no legislation of ancient times could, in its inmost spirit, be so decidedly opposed to slavery as was the Mosaic: a religion which so sharply emphasized the high dignity of man as a being made in the image of God, a legislation based upon that very idea of man's worth, and which, in all its enactments, insisted not only upon the highest justice, but also upon the tenderest pity and forbearance, especially towards the necessitous and the unfortunate ; a people, in fine, which had itself smarted under the yoke of slavery, and had become a nation only by emancipation, would necessarily be solicitous to do away, wher-

---

* Histoire des Institutions de Moise, Book VII., Chap. 7.   For this entire Chapter see Apendix A.

ever it was practicable, with the unnatural state of slavery, by which human nature is degraded."*

The wisest and best among the Jews have been accustomed to construe the Mosaic code as forbidding slavery. "Our sages," says Maimonides, "ordered us to make the poor and orphans our domestics, instead of employing slaves. . . . Every one who increases his slaves does day by day increase sin and iniquity in the world ; while those who employ the poor as their domestics [or 'sons of the house'] add hourly to their good acts." The religion of the Old Testament, in spirit and in practice, was an anti-slavery religion ; and hence, when the Jews had degenerated and had begun to practice oppression, we find their prophets threatening divine judgments for this specific wickedness, and requiring them "to break every yoke," in order. that they may escape those judgments. How impressive a warning to us is conveyed in this anti-slavery tone of Hebrew prophecy—"Rob not the poor, because he is poor : neither oppress the afflicted in the gate ; for the Lord will plead their cause, and spoil the soul of those that spoiled them."† Jehovah threatens to lay waste his vineyard, the house of Israel, because "he looked for justice, but, behold, oppression ; for righteousness, but, behold, a cry."‡ And, again, as if forecasting the judicial consequences of slavery upon our own nation, "thus saith the Holy One of Israel, Because ye despise this word, and trust in oppression, and per-

* Die Verhältnisse, etc., p. 7. Also, in Am. Theo. Review, Vol. III., p. 234. For further elucidation of this topic, see Ewald's views, in Appendix B.
† Prov. xxii. 22. ‡ Is. v. 7.

verseness, and stay thereon; therefore this iniquity shall
be to you as a breach ready to fall, swelling out in a high
wall, whose breaking cometh suddenly at an instant.
Thus saith the Lord, Ye have not hearkened unto me, in
proclaiming liberty every one to his brother, and every
man to his neighbor; behold I proclaim a liberty for you,
saith the Lord, to the sword, to the pestilence, and to the
famine."*

VII.

THE TEACHINGS OF THE APOSTLES.

Such were the principles in which the apostles as Jews
were trained; and by the working of these principles, it
had come to pass in their time that involuntary servitude
had well-nigh ceased to exist in their nation. A true
understanding of the Mosaic tenure of service is essential to right views of Christian ethics as applied to
slavery. With these humane and liberal sentiments of
the Jewish code, enforced by Christ's doctrine of neigh-
borly love, the travelling apostles came in contact with
Roman slavery as I have already described it. How did
they treat that system?

1. They had no occasion to treat, in the form of an
ethical essay, of the system of slave-laws as existing in
the Roman empire; for they had no such legal position
or political rights as could invite them to that mode of

---

* Is. xxx. 12, 13. Jer. xxxiv. 17.

treating any public or social question. They published no treatise upon the infamous domestic code of Rome, by which the father had the power of life and death over the son, and the husband power to inflict corporeal punishment upon the wife, and even death itself. They published no treatise against the cruel and depraving spectacles of the gladiatorial arena. Does Christianity therefore sanction the act of Titus in giving two thousand Jews to the wild beasts at Beyrout, or approve a modern Spanish bull-fight? The collective epistles of the New Testament were originally separate manuscript letters to little companies of obscure believers, here and there, in the Roman empire. They could be multiplied only by hand, and there was no way in which they could be brought to bear upon public sentiment, except through the enlightened and rectified sentiment of these believers.

But through these, the apostles attack slavery in the concrete so as utterly to forbid chattelism in the church of Christ. In that church the law of equality is asserted throughout the New Testament: "One is your master, even Christ, and all ye are brethren." Let me here repeat a course of argument published years ago, and still unanswered:

Christians were a peculiar people. They formed a spiritual society apart from the world, and were fellow-citizens of that commonwealth. In this relation they ceased to be under the Roman law as their source of right or rule of action. Hence the relation of master and servant was at once lifted out of the plane of the civil law into the higher plane of Christian love. The outward relation constituted by law might not cease ; it might not be possible always or at once legally to terminate this ; but chattelism, which is the essence of slavery, was abolished by the fundamental law of Christianity.

See how the gospel transforms this Roman chattel into a Christian man : *"Masters, render to your servants that which is just and equal."* Treat them as your equals in all the essential rights of men—as husbands, as fathers, ,as laborers worthy of their hire, as rational and immortal souls, give to them EQUALITY.* These words are the death-blow of Roman chattel-slavery. They are good where slavery does not exist—for every relation of master and servant ; but they abolish slavery at a stroke.

* Rev. Dr. Hodge, of Princeton, whose learning and orthodoxy none will dispute, and whom none will accuse of "abolitionism," thus comments on this passage in his work on Ephesians :

"*Give to your servants that which is just and equal.* That is, act towards them on the principles of justice and equality. Justice requires that all their rights as men, as husbands, and as parents, should be regarded. And these rights are not to be determined by the civil law, but by the law of God. 'As the law,' says Calvin, 'gave great license to masters, many assumed that everything was lawful which the civil statute allowed ; and such was their severity that the Roman emperors were obliged to restrain their tyranny. But although no edicts of princes interposed in behalf of the slave, God concedes nothing to the master beyond what the law of love allows.' Paul requires for slaves not only what is strictly just, but τὴν ἰσότητα. What is that? Literally, it is *equality*. This is not only its signification, but its meaning. Slaves are to be treated by their masters on the principles of equality. Not that they are to be equal with their masters in authority or station, or circumstances ; but *they are to be treated as having, as men, as husbands, and as parents*, EQUAL RIGHTS WITH THEIR MASTERS. It is just as great a sin to deprive a slave of the just recompense for his labor, or to keep him in ignorance, or to take him from his wife or child, as it is to act thus towards a free man. This is the equality which the law of God demands, and on this principle the final judgment is to be administered."

This command is enforced by a solemn reference to the judgment—"knowing that both your and their Master is in heaven ; *neither is there respect of persons with Him.*" And, on the other hand, the servant made free by the gospel is not to plume himself on that, nor to set himself upon his dignity ; but to be voluntarily humble and faithful in his position, not quitting a master because that master is declared to be his equal. "They that have believing masters, let them not *despise* them because they are brethren."* How could a chattel despise its owner? How does that caution sound in the ears of modern slaveholders? What Southern church would tolerate such an exhortation to its slaves?

Hear the decree of the Apostle Paul for the abolition of slavery : As many of you as have been baptized into Christ have put on Christ. You are all alike covered with Christ's righteousness and radiant with his glory. Each and every one of you is Christ. And now shall the Christ *here* oppress and injure the Christ *there?*

---

* In 1 Tim. vi. 1, 2, Paul makes a distinction between two classes of servants. First, those still "*under the yoke*," that is, having heathen masters, are to be submissive and obedient, from a regard to the honor of God. Secondly, those having "believing masters" are not to *despise* those masters, because Christianity has taken away their legal preëminence, and reduced them to a common brotherhood with their servants. Does not this argue the virtual emancipation of every slave whose master became a Christian?

The case of Onesimus is in point. He wished to return to his once legal master, whom probably he had defrauded when he ran away. Paul certifies his conversion, assumes his debts, and exhorts Philemon to receive him, "*not* now as a servant, but *above* a servant, a *brother beloved.*" For Philemon to have done otherwise would have been contrary to the gospel. Paul might have retained Onesimus, and would have done so had he not felt that Philemon could be trusted to treat him as a brother. Onesimus, if he ever was a slave, did not return as such.

Shall one soul made bright with the glory of Christ, soil
and trample under foot that glory in another? Nay, ye
have each and all put off self and put on Christ;—
there is neither Jew nor Greek—there are no favorites
in this spiritual commonwealth; there is *neither bond nor
free*—no distinctions of caste are here allowed; there is
neither male nor female—no tyranny of the stronger sex
over the weaker; there are no privileged persons or
classes whatever in this kingdom, for ye are all ONE in
Christ Jesus.

' Christianity was a kingdom within a kingdom. Pene-
trating through all forms of government and of society,
it gave its law directly to the soul; and then, working
from the individual outward, it leavened and renovated
society and its institutions. It did not work by social
revolution as a means to an end, but produced social
revolution as a necessary consequence of its transformation of the individual. But it is a great fallacy to sup-
pose that because the result to be effected by Christianity
was gradual and remote, therefore the principle tending
to that result was left to a gradual development. The
principle which should regulate society, and which in
time would reform society in the mass, was laid down
at the outset as the supreme law for the individual.

Because the process of social transformation must
needs be slow, the necessity for that transformation and
the principles by which it must be effected, were not left
to be gradually discovered in the future. No individual
was suffered to hide himself under the shadow of society :

to plead that an evil or abuse with which he was impli-
cated was a social evil that time must cure, and to take
advantage of the delay in reforming society, to indulge a
little longer his own complicity with the wrong. No;
the law that was to permeate and revolutionize society
was given *as a law* to the individual believer, the moment he entered the kingdom of God. He could not
cross the threshold of that kingdom until he bowed his
will to the supremacy of that law.*

In political affairs, the Christian of Nero's time had no
voice nor influence ; no right of suffrage, nor legislative
power. He could not therefore do anything politically
for the abolition of slavery. Moreover, at the beginning of the Christian era, the manumission of slaves,
hitherto permitted by Roman law and custom, was
greatly restricted by the *Lex Ælia Sentia* and the
Lex Fusia Caninia. But the law of Christ's kingdom
forbade one to hold as chattels men whom Christ himself had created, and had redeemed with his own precious
blood.

To sum up the argument from the New Testament,
" the Holy Scriptures lay down as absolute principles,
the equality of men before God, the lawfulness of wages,
the unity and brotherhood of the human race, the duty
of loving one another, and of loving the smallest most
of any, the obligation to do to our neighbor as we would
have him do by us. . . . . . But they preach at the
same time submission, the voluntary acceptance of the

* See the author's essay, " Teachings of the New Testament on Slavery," 1856

conditions inflicted on each one in this transient exile on earth. They radically change the title of authority and the spirit of servitude. They do not detach the slave from being a slave, they detach the master from being a master. Occupied, moreover, before everything, with the enfranchisement of souls, they seek to make of the master and the slave two brethren on earth, and of these brethren two saints in heaven. To those who suffer, they say, *Wait!* to those who inflict suffering, *Tremble!*" *

VIII.

THE FIRST THREE CENTURIES.

FROM the apostolic age of planting, we pass to the period of development, from the death of John to the conversion of Constantine ;—when Christianity as a new religion,-aiming at universal diffusion, came into collision with the religious, social, and political institutions of the pagan world. What was the first bearing of Christianity toward slavery ? and what its general influence upon the system ? Rightly to answer these questions, we must remember, first, as stated above, that, in the Roman empire, there was no such thing as popular suffrage upon public questions—and therefore Christians had no power to act politically against slavery, nor to influence the

* Cochin, Results of Slavery, p. 327.

law-making power. Next, we must remember, that at this time, Christianity itself had no recognized legal or social *status;* but its adherents were largely from the poor, and many of them slaves. And, again, we must remember, that this was one prolonged period of persecution ; marked especially by the ten great persecutions from Nero, Domitian, and Trajan, down to Diocletian ;— a period in which the church at times was compelled to hide itself in the catacombs that underlie the city of Rome, in the tombs along the valley of the Nile, and in the deserts of Egypt and Arabia.

Moreover, it was a period of which we have but meager literary remains as materials of church history. We are not therefore to look for the influence of Christianity in public laws, or in public sentiment, or in great social revolutions, or in judicial or literary monuments. Pagan writers of this period,—Tacitus and Suetonius, for example—had no conception of the genius of Christianity, and took no pains to distinguish between Christians and Jews. In fact, regarding Christians only as a pestilential sect of Jews, these authors transfer to them the hatred and contempt which so abounded toward the race of Israel. In the absence of an accurate census of the Pagan and Christian empires, respectively, it is difficult to trace the ameliorating influence of the gospel upon slavery in the interval from Augustus to Constantine. Yet we have striking evidence that in this era of oppression from without, the spirit of freedom and of equality was preserved within the Church, and that instead of

courting the patronage of the world by winking at iniquity in the rich and great, the Christians of that age
so far maintained the fundamental teachings of the gospel with regard to the essential equality of men, that
when owners of slaves became Christians, they manumitted their slaves as a preliminary to uniting with the
church.

It is not claimed that such manumission, in form, was a
pre-requisite, or a uniform preliminary to Christian fel-
lowship. The primitive Christians were not perfect,
either in the doctrines, or in the spirit and practice of the
gospel. The epistles of Paul and John rebuke doctrinal
errors, and James reproves the spirit of caste, and a regard for social distinctions in the Christian assembly.
Besides, as noted above, in the first two centuries of the
Christian era, it was the general policy of the Roman
Emperors to obstruct by legal hindrances the manumission of slaves by individual masters ;—just as in some of
the Southern States, emancipation upon the soil is embar-
rassed by regulations almost prohibitory.

It is admitted, then, that there are traces of nominal
slaveholding in the churches in post-apostolic times. Jus-
tin Martyr complains that the slaves of Christians were
put to the torture to compel them to calumniate their
masters ;* Athenagoras appeals to the slaves in Christian
households to vindicate their masters from alleged scan-
dals ;† and Eusebius mentions that heathen household
servants belonging to the brethren, being threatened with

* Apol. II., 12.   † Apology for Christianity, 35.

CHRISTIANITY AND EMANCIPATION.

the torture, at the instigation of the persecutors, charged
upon Christians the most odious vices and crimes.* But
while traces of slavery are found as an occasional residu-
um of paganism, among the early Christians, it is evident
from the tone of the Fathers, that, within the pale of the
church, "the slave passed from the category of things
which the right of property placed at the disposal of the
master."† "Slaves," said Clement of Alexandria, in the
second century, "are men like ourselves ; God is the
same for all, for slaves and for the free."‡ Cyprian, of
Carthage, in the third century, defending Christians from
false accusations, reminds his pagan adversary of the unnatural crime of slavery :—you compel to be your slave,
a man who was born as you were, who dies as you do,
whose body is made of the same substance with your own,
whose soul had the same origin with yours, who has the
same rights and is under the same law.§ That these
principles were carried into practice in the church, we
have the evidence of credible history. For though the
number of slaves set free by individual masters may be
exaggerated—as when Ovinius, of Gaul, is said to have

* Eu. Hist., V., 1. See, also, the Letter from the churches of Lyons and Vienne
to Asia, Sec. 4.
          † *Wallon: Histoire L'Esclavage*, III., 344.
‡ "Ac famulis quidem utendum est tanquam nobis ipsis; sunt enim homines
sicut nos; Deus enim est omnibus, liberis et servis, ex æquo, si consideres."—
Paedag. III., 12.
§ "Homo hominem parere tibi et obedire compéllia. Et cum sit vobis eadem
sors nascendi, conditio una moriendi, corporum materia consimilis, animarum ratio
communis, æquali jure et pari lege vel veniatur in istum mundum, vel de mundo
postmodum recedatur."—Cyp. ad. Demet. See, also, his Epistle on the duty and
privilege of redeeming captives. Epis. LXII.

as

emancipated five thousand, and Melanius eight thousand
—that very exaggeration in the popular traditions shows
the tendency of Christianity toward universal emancipation. In this view, making due allowance for the exaggeration of numbers, such instances as the following are
valuable, not only as substantial facts, but as "the expo-
nents of the spirit which animated the church at that time
concerning the duties of Christian masters."[*]

"A Roman prefect, Hermas, converted in the reign of
Trajan (98–to 117), received baptism at an Easter festi-
val, with his wife and children, and twelve hundred and
fifty slaves, and on this occasion gave all his slaves their
freedom, and munificent gifts besides. So, in the martyr-
ology of St. Sebastian, it is related that a wealthy Roman
prefect, Chromatius, under Diocletian (284–305), on
embracing Christianity, emancipated fourteen hundred
slaves, after having them baptized with himself, because
their sonship with God put an end to their servitude to
man. In the beginning of the fourth century, St. Can-
tius, Cantianus, and Cantianilla, of an old Roman family,
set all their slaves, seventy-three in number, at liberty,
after they had received baptism. After the third century,
the manumission became a solemn act, which took place
in the presence of the clergy and the congregation. The
master led the slave to the altar ; there the document of
emancipation was read, the minister pronounced the blessing, and the congregation received him as a free brother,
with equal rights and privileges. Constantine found this

custom already established, and African councils of the fourth century requested the Emperor to give it general force."

As an indication of the tone of feeling on slavery, Lactantius, in the beginning of the fourth century, writes, "Should any say : Are there not also among you poor and rich, servants and masters, distinctions among individuals ? No ; we call ourselves brethren for no other reason than that we hold ourselves all equal. For since we measûre everything human, not by its outward appearance, but by its intrinsic value, we have, notwithstanding the difference of outward relations, no slaves, but we call and consider them brethren in the spirit, and fellow-servants in religion." The same writer says : "God would have all men equal . . . . . With him there is neither servant nor master. If he is the same Father to all; they are all with the same right free. So no one is poor before God, but he who is destitute of righteousness ; no one rich but he who is full of virtues."

These noble Christian sentiments and practices found expression at last in the form of law, when Constantine embraced Christianity, and made himself the patron of the church. In the year 316, this Emperor decreed that masters wishing to free their slaves might resort to the churches, and perform the act of emancipation in presence of the congregation, with the attestation of the bishops, and that proper documents, signed by actors and witnesses, should be preserved in the church archives, for the protection of the freedman. What would those

modern evangelical Christians, whose delicate consciences
are shocked if the word slavery falls from the pulpit,
have done in such a church, and with such a gospel! Liberty was declared imprescriptible by its own nature, and,
in 322, Constantine issued a charter for the protection of
freedmen, surrounding their rights with all possible
means of defense. And thus, as the Duke de Broglie
finely says, "the church was invested with a sort of official patronage for the enfranchisement of mankind [of
whom the major part were then in slavery]. The places
consecrated to the Christian faith became the asylums of
liberty—the inviolable free soil. The church, at this solemn moment, accepted from God and from Constantine the
task of emancipating the world without overturning it."*

This imperial edict is a high and ineffaceable water-
mark by which to measure the elevation of humanity
through the gospel. To appreciate it, we must remind
ourselves again, how the later pagan emperors had imposed new restrictions upon the ancient right of manumission ; how vainly one looks for anything like common
human feeling in the Roman slave-law of republican
times, and that of the earlier empire ; how the humane
and candid historian, Tacitus, commends, as a measure
"both of justice and security," the decree of the Roman
Senate, that "if any one was killed by his slaves, not
only all his household slaves, but all under his roof who
were made free by his will, should be executed for the

* L'Englise et L'Empire Romain, I., 306.   For these laws of Constantine, see the
Code Theod. under titles.

murder ;" we must remind ourselves how, when under Nero, the prefect of the city, Pedanius Secundus, was murdered by a slave, four hundred slaves were adjudged to death ; and when the populace threatened to prevent the execution, the Senate voted that it should go forward —Caius Cassius arguing that the mixed rabble of slaves must be restrained by the utmost terrors of the law ; and through lines of soldiers awing the people, these four hundred bondmen were led to a butchery like that of Dahomey. Tacitus records this bloody holocaust of slavery, without one word of horror or of adverse criticism![*] At that time, Paul, the prisoner of the same Nero, himself in bonds at Rome, dictated by the hands of Onesimus, whom he had enfranchised in the Lord, that immortal decree of emancipation—" Masters, give unto your servants that which is just and equal ; knowing that ye also have a master in heaven :—there is neither Greek nor Jew, circumcision nor uncircumcision, barbarian, Scythian, bond nor free ; but Christ is all, and in all."[†] Well may the skeptic whom I quoted at the outset, confess his admiration of this sublime announcement. "Antiquity recognized and valued the citizen alone ; Christianity inaugurated the future of man ; Paul announces a new order of things. For the first time, man has a value as such, without distinction of race or of social condition. Jesus Christ is the Saviour of humanity ; all are called ; the slave and the master have one God ; they are brethren."[‡]

[*] Annals, XIII., 32.   [†] Col. iv. 1; iii. 11.
[‡] Laurent : *Le Christianisme*, p. 97.

Go forward now, 250 years, from Nero to Constantine—from the day when the streets of Rome were lined with soldiers to enforce the Senators' decree for the massacre of four hundred slaves in cold blood, to the day when an imperial edict makes the old basilica of despotism, converted into churches, the asylum of the slave. "Beautiful was the mission assigned to Christianity, of presiding at this act of humanity and equality ; it associated with liberty a religious idea, and announced to Christians that in the bosom of the church there should no more be masters or slaves. Every judicial act was forbidden upon the Sabbath ; but Constantine authorized the manumission of slaves," as a religious solemnity upon the Lord's day, in the house of God.*

I am far from claiming, in behalf of Constantine, an enlightened Christian consistency, and adopting the eulogy of Eusebius, that "in words, and yet more in actions, he was a herald of the truth to all mankind."† Constantine was a sagacious but not an unselfish ruler. Living in troublous times, he looked chiefly to the foundation of his throne. He would not hazard the convulsion of his empire by a decree of universal emancipation. But, although Constantine did not abolish slavery, see what he did to ameliorate the condition of slaves ;—raising the servant from a place among *things*, to the position of a *person* entitled to the protection of the law. By an edict of 312, he declared it homicide for a master maliciously to kill his slave. He gave freedom to slaves who became

* Laurent: *Christianisme*, p. 324.   † Oration, Chap. xviii.

witnesses against fraud, adultery, and other crimes. By
three successive edicts, he enacted that all slaves whose
manumission was certified by the priests, should enjoy the
freedom of Roman citizens.* In all this he may have
been influenced by mixed political motives. It may be,
as sometimes alleged, that he sought to increase the proportion of Christians in the empire, by holding forth
emancipation as a reward to slaves for the profession of
Christianity ; but this surely was a homage to the spirit
of the gospel, as approving human freedom. It was the
leaven of Christian doctrine slowly pervading the legislation of an empire that was originally based upon the
distinction of master and slave as inhering in nature itself.

IX.

SLAVERY IN THE MIDDLE AGES.

WE now enter upon the third period in the history of
our subject—stretching from Constantine to the Reformation. Here, at the outset, we encounter various new
elements in the great social problem we are attempting
to solve ; elements, some of which hindered, while others
favored the action of Christian thought and feeling in regard to slavery. First among these was the invasion of
the Roman empire by the Teutonic tribes. This irrup-
tion of northern barbarians into the empire that Chris-

* Sozomen: Ecc. Hist., L, 9. *Biot: L'Abolition de L'Esclavage,* p. 148.

4

tianity had begun to mould for the highest civilization, was like a land-slide burying an unfinished cathedral. After the first shock is over, we may trace the outline of the foundations ; here and there we find a buttress, a window, a pinnacle ; and had the building fallen of itself, we might hope to reconstruct it from its own materials ; but the mass of rubbish thrown upon it from without, the earth, trees, stones, mixed with the ruins of the structure, make it impossible ever again to fashion it as it was. Beside the universal perturbation of society caused by the barbarian invasion, and the overthrow of that regulating power which had begun to give consistency and beauty to the social structure, there was strown over the wide fall of the Roman empire, "such a confused mass of languages, customs, manners, and laws,"* that it was impossible to rear again the house as Constantine had left it. " Before the conclusion of the fifth century, the mighty fabric of empire, which valor and policy had founded upon the seven hills of Rome, was finally overthrown, in all the west of Europe, by the barbarous nations from the north."†

The invaders, ignorant, fierce, cruel, brought with them their own type of slavery, which Tacitus has described in his Germania ; and many a Christian captive was compelled to become the prædial serf of a barbarian lord. These centuries of danger, disaster, and degradation, were, as Milman says, " the time for great Christian virtues ;" and yet while modifying the Teutonic

---

* *Balmes'* Protestantism and Catholicity.   † Hallam, Middle Ages, Chap. I.

races to its own spirit, Christianity itself suffered a serious deterioration, and " began rapidly to barbarize." In the end, no doubt, the breaking up of the Roman empire and the substitution of feudal serfdom for Roman chattelism furthered the abolition of slavery. But at the first, the era of violence threatened to roll back the whole tide of progress marked by the era of Constantine. In judging of that progress in a given direction, we must keep in mind how slowly the world, as a whole, was Christianized.

The rancor of theological controversies in the Church, resulting at last in the great schism between the eastern and the western branches, tended also to arrest the influence of Christianity in the general amelioration of society. As the church lost unity of sentiment it declined also in moral force.

Still more disastrous in its bearing upon human freedom, was the gradual secularization of the church by its alliance with the State. In the growth of that central and secularized church-power at Rome which culminated in the papal supremacy, the church acquired by grants, by legacies, and even by conquest, domains upon which were serfs bound to the soil. The increase of worldly wealth and power in the church tended of course to repress its Christian activity, and especially to stifle those humane sentiments of equality and fraternity which the gospel inculcates. The apostacy of the middle ages resembled that of the Jews in the time of Isaiah ; religious ceremonies, fasts and penances were used to cover the

enormous wickedness of fraud and oppression ; church-
men and prelates became owners of slaves.

Throughout this period, therefore, we must keep in
mind the distinction between the Church and Christianity.
As Finlay well puts it, in his history of the Byzantine
empire,* "though *ecclesiastical* influence has exercised
immense authority over the internal policy of European
society, *religious* influence has always been compara-
tively small ; and though Christianity has labored to
abolish slavery, it was often for the interest of the church
tó perpetuate the institution."

But notwithstanding these adverse influences, the long
period of which we speak, even in its darkest portions,
was illumined with the testimony of leaders in the Christian church, and, also, of its corporate legislation, against
the oppression of the poor.   If we interrogate Augustine,
this great father of Christian theology, while he inter-
prets the Apostle Paul as having "set the master over
the slave, and put the slave under the master," in their
temporal relations, nevertheless reminds masters that
"Christ gave the same price for both."†   Wherefore he
says, "it is not meet that a Christian should possess a
slave in the same way that he possesses a horse or
money."‡   Again, in preaching on the Lord's prayer, he
says, "Under our Father in heaven the Lord and the
slave are brethren ; under this Father the general and

---

* Vol. I., p. 261.   † Sermon XLIV.

‡ De Serm. in Mont. Matt. v. 40. "Non enim Christianum oportet sic possidere
servum, quomodo equum aut argentum.

the common soldier are brethren ; under this Father the rich and the poor are brethren."*

Said Gregory of Nyssa (died 394), "God said, Let us make man in our image. Him who is made in the likeness of God, who rules over the whole earth, who is clothed by God with power over all things upon the earth ; tell me, who is it that sells or buys such an one? . . . How shall that be sold which is above the whole world and all that it contains? For it is necessary also to sell his faculties ; and at what price will you estimate the mind of man, that rules the world? Though you should name the whole world, you will not have told its price : for he who knows man hath said, that the whole world is not enough to give in exchange for the soul. When, therefore, a man is exposed for sale, nothing less is brought into the market than the lord of the earth." How would Richmond or Charleston endure the gospel at the mouth of Augustine or Gregory? Is anti-slavery preaching a modern political device?

Gregory goes on to argue the equality of masters and servants: "They have the same affections of mind and of body ; the same joy and sorrow, the same pleasure and pain, the same anger and fear, and are subject to the same sickness and death. They breathe the same air, behold the same sun, have the same vital organs, are nourished by the same food. After death, master and slave become alike dust; they stand before the same

---

* Sermon IX., on the Lord's Prayer.

judge; their heaven and their hell are the same."* How
long would such a preacher of the gospel be tolerated in
New Orleans?

St. Isidore, of Pelusium (440), urges that servants
should be treated even as ourselves, because they are
men like ourselves. Against the plea that they are subjected to others by the fortune of war, or by superior
force, he insists that "in reality we are but one with
them, whether by agreement of nature, or by the principles of our faith, or in view of the last judgment."† Again
he says, "*I know not how a man who loves Christ—who
has known and experienced that grace which has secured
freedom for us all—can hold a slave.*"‡ Is opposition
to slavery a fanaticism of modern times?

There is a touching legend of St. Bavon, that long after
he had renounced the world for a monastic life, he met
a man whom he had once sold as a slave, when, falling at
his feet he begged his forgiveness for the great crime he
had committed, and offered to submit to any degradation
or penance his injured victim would impose.

The legend shows the tone of popular feeling in regard
to slavery. To repent of slaveholding as a crime, and to
offer reparation to the victim, were deemed meritorious

---

* See the whole of this masterly sermon in the works of Gregory, p. 406.

† Servis, tanquam nobis ipsis, utendum est. Homines enim illi nostri instar
sunt. Anticipata quippe opinio, aut belli fortuna, aut armorum vis, eos in aliorum
possessionem redigit. At re vira omnes unum utque idem sumus, sive naturam,
sive fidem, sive futurum judicium spectemus."

‡ In his epistle to Ironis: "Neque enim Christi amantem Ironem, qui cognitam et
exploratam eam gratiam habeat, qui omnes in libertatem vindicavit, famulum
ullum habere arbitror."

acts in a saint. All these declarations are based upon the incompatibility of slavery with the idea of man as the offspring of God and as redeemed by the precious blood of Christ.

These generous sentiments of the Christian fathers find a partial echo in legislation, especially in the Byzantine empire—though we should no more judge of Christianity in that age by the character and decrees of nominal Christian emperors, than we would judge of Christianity in England by the character and demands of her Tudors and Stuarts as defenders of the faith. In the code of Justinian are various enactments ameliorating the condition of slaves, reducing their number, favoring the enfranchisement of individuals, and restraining the cruelty of masters, though there is an obvious design to conserve and regulate the system of slavery rather than to abolish it. But while we recognize in the humane features of this celebrated code the softening influences of Christianity upon imperial despotism, we surely cannot charge upon the gospel the lack of wisdom, of courage, or of piety in an emperor called Christian.

A more decisive proof of the anti-slavery influence of Christianity is given in frequent acts and declarations of councils, convents, bishops, popes, the ecclesiastical representatives of the middle ages. In the sixth century, we see the pious Gregory with his own purse ransoming Saxon slaves brought for sale to Rome, and educating them to become missionaries to barbarian Britain. As pope, he used his authority for the protection of the erslaved; and there is extant a letter manumitting two persons who had been his own slaves, which marks at once the noble piety of the man and the evangelical spirit of the time. "As our Redeemer, the Author of all beings, has been pleased to put on the human form to break by the grace of his divinity the bonds which held us captive, and to restore to us our former liberty, it is fitting and salutary that those whom nature has made free, and whom human law has subjected to the yoke of servitude, should be restored by the boon of enfranchisement to the liberty in which they were born." Moved by this consideration, and as a dictate of piety, he formally renounces all claim to the service of these servants of God and of his church.*

In the eighth century we find the heads of convents giving freedom to all slaves received with lands bestowed upon the monastery. The head of one of these institutions writes, "a monk should never possess a slave, either for his own service or for the service of the convent, or to cultivate its lands; for *the slave is a man created in the image of God.*"†

---

* The following is the original of this epistle: "Cum Redemptor noster totius conditor creaturæ ad hoc propitiatus humanam voluerit carnem assumere, ut divinitatis suæ gratia, diruto quo tenebamur captivi vinculo servitutis, pristinæ nos restitueret libertati; salubriter agiter, si homines quos ab initio natura creavit liberos et protulit, et jus gentium jugo substituit servitutis, in ea natura in qua nati fuerant, manumittentis beneficio, libertati reddantur. Atque ideo pietatis intuitu, et hujus rei consideratione permoti, vos Montanam atque Thomam famulos sanctæ Romanæ Ecclesiæ, cui Deo adjutore deservimus, liberos ex hac die civesque Romanos efficimus, omnequo vestrum vobis relaxamus servitutis peculium." (Greg. I., v. Ep. xii.) See, also, the acts of various Councils, in Appendix C.

† Theodore Studita.

An early English bishop received of the king of Sussex 250 slaves with land ; he at once baptized them and set them free. In 1102, a church council, at London, condemned the slave trade—"that wicked traffic, by which men of England have been sold like brute animals ;" and a little later, at the council of Armagh, in Ireland, "the bishops declared that the misfortunes of their country were the just punishment of the perpetuated crime of slavery," and freed all captives held as slaves. A bull of Pope Gregory XVI. interdicts all ecclesiastics from "venturing to maintain that the traffic in blacks is permitted under any pretext whatever ; and from teaching in public or in private, or in any way whatever, anything to the contrary." Between the third and the twelfth centuries, no less than thirty-seven public councils of the church rendered decisions for the relief of slaves. During four centuries not a council met which did not denounce the slave-trade and urge its abolition ; and in the twelfth century slavery had well-nigh died out of Europe as under the ban of Christianity.* It became a common thing for the faithful to emancipate their slaves as an act of merit, for the salvation of their own souls and the souls of their ancestors. Penitents would even buy slaves in order to manumit them in the church ; and the Bible was set upon the head of the freed man as a crown of liberty.

The slave made free could rise to any office or dignity in the church. When a king of Hungary, in the thirteenth century, complained to Gregory IV., that a bishop

* See Appendix C.

was of servile origin, the Pope answered, "Before God all men are equal." There was a doctrine of human rights before the French Revolution, before Thomas Jefferson. All honor to Popes and councils who, in the dark ages, held up this great light of liberty.* Of this whole period Guizot says, "the clergy in general, and especially several popes, enforced the manumission of their slaves as a duty incumbent upon laymen, and loudly inveighed against the scandal of keeping Christians in bondage. The greater part of the forms by which slaves were set free, at various epodes, are founded upon religious motives. It is under the impression of some religious feeling—the hopes of the future, the equality of all Christian men, and so on—that the freedom of the slave is granted. These are rather convincing proofs of the influence of the church, and of her desire for the abolition of this evil of evils, this iniquity of iniquities."*

X.

ANTI-SLAVERY IN MODERN TIMES.

BUT such an evil dies hard. It is like the banyan, whose branches strike down again to the soil that nurses it, and become the stocks of other trees. And so in

---

*For conclusive evidence on these points, see *Balmes'* "Protestantism and Catholicity," especially the original citations in the appendix: *Biot*, "Abolition de L'Esclavage;" *Cochin*, "Results of Slavery;" and above all, the great work of *Wallon*, "Histoire de L'Esclavage."

† History of Civilization.

the fifteenth and sixteenth centuries, slavery which had
been cut down and thinned out, but not extirpated,
began to sprout again, and in the seventeenth century it
was fostered by European sovereigns, in the interest of
colonies and of commerce.

For a time, the Reformers had so much to do in the
way of conflict and of suffering, to win for Protestantism
a recognized position and field of action in Europe, that
they could give but little time to philanthropic reform,
and, indeed, could have but little influence toward social
and legal reformations. But there stood the gospel, de-
claring all men made of one blood, children of one father,
redeemed by one Saviour; there stood the sermon on
the Mount, the parable of the good Samaritan, the golden
rule of equal justice and fraternal love; there stood the
teachings of the Apostles and the practice of the early
church; and this gospel testimony must be heard again.
By degrees it found a voice, first through individual
Christians, then by combined Christian action, and
through the reformation of laws. Of this more recent
anti-slavery agitation, I need not speak in detail. Bishop
Warburton and Bishop Porteus, Bishop Horsley, and
Archdeacon Paley, Bishop Butler and John Wesley, and
many other illustrious names of England, are enrolled in
the list of witnesses against the crime of slavery. I need
barely refer to the testimony of Hopkins of Newport,
and Edwards of New Haven; to the consistent anti-
slavery testimony of the Society of Friends; of the somewhat fluctuating and inconsistent, and yet in the main,

the emphatic and earnest protests of other Christian bodies in this land, against our monster iniquity. Whatever the delinquencies of individual ministers and churches in this regard, in proportion to the vitality of religion in the land has been its effect in toning the public conscience against slavery.

The abolition of the slave trade and of slavery in the British Parliament, was led by Christian men on Christian grounds. After his first failure, Wilberforce wrote : "I never felt so on any Parliamentary occasion. I could not sleep. The poor blacks rushed into my mind, and the guilt of our wicked land. I do not deserve the signal honour of being an instrument of putting an end to this atrocious and unparalleled wickedness. But, O Lord, let me earnestly pray thee to pity these children of affliction, and to terminate their unequal wrongs."* That is the spirit of the Christian. Having witnessed the abolition of the slave-trade, in later life Wilberforce urges Buxton to enter upon the blessed service of abolishing slavery. Buxton's motion in Parliament was " that the state of slavery is repugnant to the British constitution and to the Christian religion." Slavery was abolished in European Christendom by the prayers and faith of Christian men.

We do not claim the whole of this work for Christianity by its direct and positive influence upon society. Slavery is so clearly against the will of God in the constitution of mankind, that natural religion is opposed to

* Anti-Slavery in Modern Times.

it in proportion to the enlightenment of reason and conscience. Even Aristotle, after all his special pleading
for slavery as a state of nature, makes this concession :
"As other men became worse when they get nothing for
being better, and when no rewards are given for virtuous
or vicious actions, so it is with slaves. . . . It is necessary
also that in everything some end should be defined ; it is
therefore right and expedient that freedom should be proposed to them [the slaves] as a reward ; for they will be
willing to labor when a prize and a definite space of time
is laid down. It is right also to bind them as hostages
by their families."*

Hence, with the progress of civilization, and the development of a public conscience and of the spirit of
personal freedom, came an intenser antagonism to slavery.
But to ascribe this, as do Laurent and Salvador to the
philosophy and the political theories of the French Revolution, is to mistake an effect for the cause. The doctrine
of political liberty and fraternity was itself an offshoot
of Christianity—the Christianity of the New Testament
as distinguished from the ecclesiasticism of the middle
ages. The leaven of Christ's teachings produced the
political fermentations of the eighteenth century as truly
as the religious fermentations of the sixteenth. When-
ever Christianity has had its legitimate expression, it has
told against slavery. As Macaulay states it, " the forms
in which Christianity has been at different times dis-
guised, have been often hostile to liberty. But wherever

* Aristotle Economics, B. I, c. v.

the spirit has surmounted the forms—in France, during the wars of the Huguenots; in Holland, during the reign of Philip II.; in Scotland, at the time of the Reformation; in England, through the whole contest against the Stuarts, from their accession to their expulsion; in New England, through its whole history—in every place—in every age—it has inspired a hatred of oppression, and a love of freedom."* Before the abolition of slavery in the British West Indies, it was made a charge against a Wesleyan missionary that he had read an inflammatory chapter of the Bible to his congregation!

XI.

SUMMARY AND CONCLUSION.

THE slave trade was abolished in 1808 by the United States; in 1811, by Denmark, Portugal, and Chili; in 1813, by Sweden; in 1814 and 1815 by Holland; in 1815 by France; the Congress of Vienne sought to obtain the entire and final abolition of a traffic so odious and so loudly reproved by the laws of religion and nature. In 1822, Spain abolished the slave trade, and in the same year Wilberforce attacked slavery, after the slave trade, and won over public opinion by appeals and repeated meetings, while his friend, Mr. Buxton, proposed emancipation in parliament. The Emancipation Bill was pre-

* Works, Vol. VI., p. 312.

sented in 1833.   On the 1st of August, 1834, slavery
ceased to sully the soil of the English colonies.   In
1846, Sweden, in 1847, Denmark, Uruguay, Wallachia
and Tunis obeyed the same impulse, which France followed in 1848, Portugal in 1856, and which Holland
has lately imitated.

Lastly, in 1861, the last form of servitude disappeared
in Russia ; and Spain, in retaking a part of the island of
St. Domingo, promised never to reëstablish slavery there.

As Cochin, whom we here follow, well puts it, "in a
century, the initiative of Wilberforce has put slavery to
rout, or at least called it in question over the whole sur-
face of Christendom ;" leaving only Spain and Brazil, and
the Southern United States as the accomplices of this iniquity.   "The destinies of servitude and liberty," he
continues, "are both at stake in the crisis which is shak-
ing the new world.   This combat is the rudest of all, but
it will be the last.   Instead of suffering one's self to be
overwhelmed by the inconceivable slowness of moral
progress, it is precisely because the last effort is difficult
that it is necessary to enter into it with all one's might,
full of faith in the sure triumph of the Christian religion,
justice, and perseverance over the conspiracy of inter-
ests, the obstinacy of prejudices, the despotic torpor of
habits."

Already Missouri leads the way to this bright and
blessed consummation ;—Missouri, that, in 1820, led us
into the fatal demoralization of slave compromises—
Missouri, that inaugurated civil war in Kansas in order

to force slavery upon her soil, now makes haste to free
herself of its curse. And that majestic Providence before which we stand in awe at each unfolding of its won-
drous plan, is causing the wrath of man to praise Him,
who hath arisen for the crying of the needy. How long
the President and his advisers held back from any official
recognition of justice and freedom for the slave as the
controlling elements in our national struggle! But at
length came that great golden day of the Proclamation.

WASHINGTON, January 1, 1863.

By the President of the United States of America :

A PROCLAMATION.   ,

WHEREAS, on the twenty-second day of September, in the year
of our Lord one thousand eight hundred and sixty-two, a proclamation was issued by the President of the United States, contain-
ing among other things the following, to wit :

"That on the first day of January, in the year of our Lord one
thousand eight hundred and sixty-three, all persons held as slaves
within any state or designated part of a state, the people whereof
shall then be in rebellion against the United States, shall be thence-
forth and *forever* FREE, and the executive government of the United
States, including the military and naval authorities thereof, will
recognize and maintain the freedom of such persons, and will do no
act or acts to repress such persons, or any of them, in any effort
they may make for their actual freedom. That the Executive will,
on the first day of January aforesaid, by proclamation, designate the
states and parts of states, if any, in which the people therein respectively shall then be in rebellion against the United States, and the
fact that any state, or the people thereof, shall on that day be, in
good faith, represented in the Congress of the United States by
members chosen thereto at elections, wherein a majority of the quali-
fied voters of such states shall have participated, shall, in the absence

of strong countervailing testimony, be deemed conclusive evidence that such states and the people thereof are not in rebellion against the United States;"

Now, therefore, I, Abraham Lincoln, President of the United States, by virtue of the power in me vested as Commander-in-Chief of the Army and Navy of the United States in time of actual armed rebellion against the authority and government of the United States, and as a fit and necessary war measure for suppressing said rebellion, do, on this first day of January, in the year of our Lord one thousand eight hundred and sixty-three, and in accordance with my purpose so to do, publicly proclaimed for the full period of one hundred days from the day of the first above-mentioned order, designate, as the states and parts of states wherein the people thereof respectively are this day in rebellion against the United States, the following, to wit:

Arkansas, Texas, Louisiana, except the parishes of St. Bernard, Placquemines, Jefferson, St. John, St. Charles, St. James, Excelsior, Assumption, Terre Bonen, Latourch, St. Mary, St. Martin and Orleans, including the city of New Orleans; Mississippi, Alabama, Florida, Georgia, South Carolina, North Carolina, and Virginia, except the forty-eight counties designated as West Virginia, and also the counties of Berkley, Accomac, Northampton, Elizabeth City, York, Princess Ann and Norfolk, including the cities of Norfolk and Portsmouth, and which excepted parts are, for the present, left precisely as if this proclamation were not issued.

And, by virtue of the power and for the purpose aforesaid, *I do order and declare that all persons held as slaves within said designated states and parts of states are and henceforward shall be* FREE. And that the Executive government of the United States, including the military and naval authorities thereof, *will recognize and maintain the freedom of said persons.*

And I hereby enjoin upon the people so declared to be free to abstain from all violence unless in necessary self-defence, and I recommend to them, that in all cases, when allowed, they labor faithfully for reasonable wages.

And I further declare and make known that *such persons of suita-*

5

ble condition will be received into the armed service of the United States, to garrison forts, positions, stations, and other places, and to man vessels of all sorts in said service.

And, upon this, sincerely believed to be an act of justice, warranted by the constitution, upon military necessity, I invoke the considerate judgment of mankind, and the gracious favor of Almighty God.

In witness whereof, I have hereunto set my hand, and caused the seal of the United States to be affixed.

Done at the city of Washington, this first day of January, in the year of our Lord one thousand eight hundred and [SEAL] sixty-three, and of the independence of the United States of America the eighty-seventh.

ABRAHAM LINCOLN.

By the President :

WM. H. SEWARD, *Secretary of State.*

It seems as if this nation, which had so long lain under the disgrace of injustice and oppression, and which, startled by the shock of war, had been blindly staggering in its old mire and chains, was then of a sudden uplifted to some granite mountain whence, above all fogs and clouds and storms, it looks out upon its long future of peace, prosperity, honor, and grandeur. The slave heard that Proclamation, and blessed God for the day. The master heard it, and replied with threats of savage cruelty and cowardice. Europe heard it, and her governments said, "no recognition of the South ;" and her people shouted Amen, Hallelujah,

But this grand and blessed act summons us to momentous duties.

1. We owe it to the honor of the gospel, to bear our un-

reserved and unanimous testimony against slavery, and to use all feasible means for its utter abolition. I have vindicated Christianity, in its principles and its history, from the aspersion of sanctioning slavery ; *we*, too, in this our time, must honor the gospel by applying it in all the strength of its precepts, in all the power of its spirit, for the extermination of slavery from the land. The war does not accomplish this work ; it prepares the way. The proclamation opens the door, and we must enter in and make the work sure. Emancipation is not abolition. Until there shall be a complete abolition of slavery, only military occupation can secure the freedom of the emancipated slaves.* Should the war stop short of uprooting slavery and reconstructing society, some new converts to anti-slavery doctrine will apostatize from their faith to their old prejudices. But the true Christian will feel then more than ever the need of earnest hostility to this iniquity. There are those whose opposition to slavery did not originate in a military necessity. For one, I am opposed to slavery because I am a Christian—a member of that anti-slavery society of which He who came to preach liberty to the captive is the founder and the head. With Cochin, I would say, "*I owe to Christianity the horror with which slavery inspires me.*"

2. We owe it to the safety and welfare of our country to sustain, and if need be to invigorate, the government in it measures for the extermination of slavery. The question is no longer one of theory but of fact ; no longer of

* See Appendix D.

the future, but of to-day ; no longer a question of expe-
diency, but of necessity ; no longer a question of man's
judgment, but a demand of God's providence. Most
truly does the President declare that "without slavery
rebellion would never have existed, without slavery it
could not continue." And we may add that the spirit of
rebellion can never be quelled, nor the tendency to vio-
lent outbreak allayed, till slavery is done away. As
Gen. Butler said to the people of New Orleans, "There
is but one thing that at this hour stands between you and
thé government, and that is slavery. The institution,
cursed of God, which has taken its last refuge here, in
His providence will be rooted out as the tares from the
wheat, although the wheat be torn up with it. I have
given much thought to this subject. I came among you,
by teachings, by habit of mind, by political position, by
social affinity, inclined to sustain your domestic laws, if
by possibility they might be with safety to the Union.
Months of experience and of observation have forced the
conviction that the existence of slavery is incompatible
with the safety either of yourselves or of the Union. As
the system has gradually grown to its present huge dimen-
sions, it were best if it could be gradually removed ; but
it is better, far better, that it should be taken out at once
than that it should longer vitiate the social, political, and
family relations of your country. I am speaking with no
philanthropic views as regards the slave, but simply of
the effect of slavery on the master. See for yourselves.
Look around you and say whether this saddening, dead-

ening influence has not all but destroyed the very frame-
work of your society." But for Christians there is a
higher point of view. God has a controversy with us,
as a nation, for aiding and abetting this sin, and he is
commanding us with a voice that shakes both earth and
heaven, "to break every yoke, and let the oppressed go
free."

3. But, in the contemplation of this vast interest we are
more than Americans—we are men ; and we owe it
to humanity to seek the full emancipation' of all the
oppressed, and their industrial, social, and moral elevation. This is preëminently the work of the gospel in this
land and in our time. Not the degradation of the old
pagan world as spread before the early Christians, not
the barbarism of the Northern hordes, as brought to the
doors of the church of the fifth century; not the ignorance,
superstition, and immorality of Europe, as these lay before the Reformers ; not the wants and woes of heathen-
dom inciting to modern missions, presented such a call
of duty, such a field of endeavor, such a promise of success, as this race upon our soil now coming out of bondage. We must build them up into society from the foundation. "Slavery is, above everything, the negation of
the family. Man is endowed with an astonishing capacity
for suffering. He knows how to live under ground, or on
the water ; an Indian in the forests, a Chinaman in his
boat, a Laplander in his darkness ; but on condition of being able to say my wife, my child, my mother, my boat,
my cabin, my tools. The slave is without family. He is

not sure of keeping his wife, or of knowing his father; his canoe is not his own ; and when he lays his hand on his breast, he cannot say, This skin is mine. Now, without these rights, the man is not a man, nature is violated in his person. Follow slavery under all latitudes, in all regions, whatever the institutions, nations, or creeds, everywhere you find the same origin, the same progress, the same law, the same result, as monotonous and horrible as the life of the slaves. The history of slavery knows no change. It is in all places, it has been at every epoch, an obstacle to the systematic peopling of the earth, an obstacle to the propagation of the gospel, an obstacle to the quiet elevation of the inferior races, an obstacle to the progressive civilization of the superior races. The moralist calls it a crime—the historian and economist a scourge.*

There is, then, no peace, no safety, no hope for us as a people, with slavery in the land. Not freedom only, but our very Christianity would go down before its blighting power. I speak not to politicians and partisans, but to Christian men and women, to those who love the gospel, who love men for whom Christ died, who love their country as the heritage and home of a Christian freedom and civilization. To you, I say, is given the future of this land, and the future of an unhappy race, to save the one by instructing and elevating the other. To you it is given to redeem Christianity from reproach, and to make it the renovating and conservative power in our convulsed and imperiled nation.

* Cochin: Results of Emancipation.

APPENDIX.

—•••—

˙X

APPENDIX A.

THE FOLLOWING IS THE CHAPTER FROM SALVADOR, ENTITLED, "DOMES-
TICITY; OR, SERVANTS IMPROPERLY CALLED SLAVES."

IT cannot be questioned that the new era, the grand period
which opened in France in the days of the Constituent Assembly,
rehdered general the cause of rational liberty to which England
had already accorded a local homage ; it cannot, I say, be questioned that this age has the honor of having really destroyed
slavery. Without doubt former times had propagated the principle ; but the philosophical era has established the fact, and it has
already advanced farther on this question, in forty years, than in
the seventeen hundred and ninety-nine years of the preceding
period.

This remark has important bearings upon the laws and statutes
of which I am to treat.

To give the means of subsistence to individuals who from one
fiftieth year to another, or from one jubilee to another, might have
alienated their property, and in order to bind closely servants to
families and families to servants, Moses made special laws upon
domesticity ; he established a contract of engagement or a lease
of service of two kinds, the septenary and the jubilary.

Now, in respect to these statutes, the received French translations of the Pentateuch furnish one of the gravest proofs of the
abuse which words or homonyms may undergo in the transition

from one language to another. Without any regard to the nature of the fact, servants, the Hebrew domestics, have been entirely transformed into *slaves*.

Perhaps, also, as I have already remarked, there has been a pious intention to let it be believed that in the law of Moses slavery was maintained, and that it is owing exclusively to the law of Jesus Christ that the earth is now rid of it.

When a Hebrew, driven by necessity, consented to serve a family—"*sold* himself as a *slave*," say the translations,—the law required the following conditions in his favor : 1*st*, as the price of his lease of engagement (or, if you please, as the price of purchase of the so-called *slave*), he received in advance a sum proportionate to the nature of the work for which he was fitted ; 2*d*, after six years, his contract of hiring, his lease of service, expired *by right ;* 3*d*, during this time he was supported, suitably maintained, and subjected to a moderate labor ; 4*th*, finally, at the expiration of his lease, he received either in money or in subsistence, sufficient to defray his expenses and the cost of returning to his paternal home.

"If thou *obtain for a servant* a Hebrew," said the law, " he shall serve thee six years, and in the seventh year he shall go free, without owing thee anything ; on the contrary, . . . when thou shalt send him away free from thee, it shall not be with empty hands : but thou shalt give him something of thy flock, of thy threshing-floor, of thy wine-press, of all that in which the Lord shall have blessed thee. During the days of his service thou shalt abstain from ruling over him rigorously, from using him as it is the custom in other places (in Egypt for example) to use slaves : he shall be to thee as the (free) hired servant and as the foreign workman."*

If the servant was happy with his master, and *loved* him, or if for reasons which will be shown hereafter, he formally desired to

---

* Deut. xv. 12. Lev. xxv. 39, 41.

remain with him, then the transition was effected from the septenary lease of which the duration was fixed, to the jubilee lease,
which was longer or shorter in proportion to the time which yet
remained before the fiftieth official year or succeeding jubilee. In
this case the custom was to lead the servant before the judges to
take action according to his wish. The end of his ear was
pierced ; this was the sign which declared that he would serve *for
ever ;* in other words, that he had renounced his lease of six years,
and that his engagement carried him·to the great year, when he
returned of right to his possession in his father's house.*

This manner of regarding servants explains at once the strange
and enormous abuse of language into which translators have fallen
when they have stated, among other things, that a Hebrew could
sell his daughter as a *slave.*

According to the law and the later regulations, before a father
could put a daughter. under age to *service,* he must be reduced to
the greatest state of distress, he must have sold all, even to his
last garment. He could not engage a daughter who had reached
the age of puberty, because then paternal authority had come to
an end, and it only remained to exercise a surveillance until the
time of marriage. The first money which the father acquired must
be used to redeemed the hired daughter—to avail himself of the
right of breaking the engagement.

Finally, and this was the grand feature of the law, the man
who took as a servant a girl in her *minority,* contracted a tacit
obligation to marry her when she should be marriageable, or
to marry her to one of his sons ; so that the virtue of a young
and perhaps beautiful girl, should not be exposed to the powerful
seductions of a master.

" When a man shall have engaged his daughter as a *servant,* it
is said, she shall not go forth from the house of her master as
other servants go forth ; if she displeases this master and he does

* Deut. xv. 17. Lev. xxv. 4.

not wish to marry her, she shall be as if released from her engagement, or redeemed, and he shall have no right to make her enter
into the service of a strange family; he cannot practice in this
respect the least deceit. If, on the contrary, he affiances her to
his son, she shall be treated according to the ordinary right of
daughters."*

When a Hebrew took his wife with him into the service of his
patron, he took her home again in the seventh year, as well as the
children whom she had borne. If he married a woman given by
his master, he went forth alone, that is to say, the woman finished
her engagement, and the children followed the fate of their mother.

The law, in this connection, leaves no doubt. It speaks of the
engagement and the lease of service by women exactly as of the
lease of service by men : " When one of thy brethren," it says,
" shall have engaged himself to thee to serve thee (shall have *sold*
himself to thee), whether he be a Hebrew man or a Hebrew
woman, he shall serve thee six years ; but in the seventh year he
shall go free." Consequently, if the sixth year of the husband
corresponded to the second year of the wife, she must still pass
four years with the master unless she redeemed or released herself. But if the wife of this man was engaged till the jubilee
year, and if he had not the means to redeem her, the master could
not refuse to keep him himself, if he asked it, till the time of general liberty.†

Foreigners or their children could hire themselves in the same
way ; for though the law says, they *shall serve for ever*, this
does not mean a real perpetuity, as is proved by the articles of
Exodus and Deuteronomy where these words are applied to the
Hebrew servant. The only difference was that the foreigner engaged for the whole jubilee-lease was required to fulfil his time of
service even to the end, while the Hebrew hired to a foreign resi-

---

* Ex. xxi. 7, 9. *Mischna*, Tom. III., *de Uxore adulter suspectâ*, chap. iii. § 5, p. 226.
† Ex. xxi. 6.

dent retained the right of ransom under conditions which will presently be indicated.* If the law adds, in regard to foreign servants, "You shall have them for a heritage and shall leave them to your children," it is in order that at the death of the master the engagement, in case it had not expired, should remain in force for his natural heirs.†

As to the manner of treating these servants taken from among the natives, it was in every respect the same as was required toward the home-born. Moses had already announced this principle: "You shall love the strangers who dwell with you, as you love yourselves;" and in a given instance, in prescribing kindness toward the Hebrew servant, he gave this injunction to the master, "Thou shalt not oppress him, but he shall be to thee as the hired servant and the stranger."‡

I will not affirm that the fundamental principle of the jubilee was extended to men sold by foreign nations, to captives, to real slaves, while reciprocity was not exercised by other nations. However, of right, the very wording of the law involved this application or was capable of receiving it. In fact, the general liberty of the year of jubilee was proclaimed neither for the benefit of the Hebrews alone nor for the benefit of affiliated foreigners; it embraced all the inhabitants of the country without distinction; it was in a sense from the sacred soil itself, that this liberty was derived. The reader can judge of this; "In the fiftieth year, ye shall proclaim liberty in the land for *all its inhabitants; each man* shall return to his possession, *every person* to his family." The lawgiver chooses the most general expressions that could be employed. This universal application of the law, beside being rightfully inferred upon such grounds, was altogether worthy of the lawgiver who had said, "When a slave shall take refuge with thee, thou shalt not return him to his master; thou shalt let him dwell in whichever of thy cities pleases him, and thou shalt not oppress

* Lev. xxv. 47–50.   † Lev. xxv. 42, 44, 45.   ‡ Lev. xxv. 40.

him." It was worthy of the man who reminded the people without ceasing, " That the greatest blessing of Jehovah toward them
consisted in having brought them out of the house of bondage."
' Independently of the term fixed by the law, the engagement for
domesticity was canceled in three ways. By the will of the master who said to the servant, " Be freed or disengaged, I give thee
thy liberty," and he gave him a deed of it. By ransom ; then the
servant repaid the money received in advance for his services, sub-
tracting from the sum the price of the time that he had worked,
and giving proof that this money had not been unjustly acquired
at the expense of another.* Finally, when the master had mal-
treated his servants to the extent of wounding them, the magis-
'trates suddenly broke the engagement and left to the servants the
integral price without detriment from the censures or penalties to
be pronounced against the guilty.†

In truth, a concluding article of this law, too concise, and in
which, perhaps, some words have been omitted, has given to the
legislator intentions which contradict all the preceding statutes of
the law. "If any one striking his man-servant or his maid-servant
wounds his eye, or occasions him any other evil of this kind, he
shall send him free immediately, to compensate him ; if he kills

* Not only does the law relative to this defalcation combine all the other statutes,
but it is well to reproduce it literally because of the new light which it sheds on
the condition of a stranger among the ancient people. "If the stranger from abroad,'
it says, " or even a resident stranger is enriched by thee, and if thy brother having
become poor *by him* engages himself to this resident stranger or to a branch of a
foreign family, there may be redemption in his favor. One of his brothers may
redeem him, or his uncle, or the son of his uncle, or any other of his near relations,
or himself if he finds the means. Then he shall reckon with his master from the
year of his engagement to the year of jubilee. If the number of years is still
great, he shall return in his ransom an equivalent part of the price of his engagement ; if there remain a few years, he shall return according to the lesser number.
He shall be regarded as a hired servant who hires himself from year to year. But
if the opportunity for his redemption does not occur, he shall go out in the year of
jubilee, he and his sons with him."—Lev. xxv. 47-54.

† *Mischna.* iii, *de Sponsalib,* chap. I, *Selden,* de Jur. nat. et gent. lib. iv. Ex.
xxi. 26, 27.

him by the blow, he is punished by death ; but if the servant dies after a day or two, the master shall not be punished with death,—it is his money.*

In this last case the law does not attribute the death of the servant to violence, since in the first it punished the guilty. These vague words, it *is his money*, express rather that the citizen is already punished by the loss sustained. If the legislator had wished to give him absolute power would he not have said ; if he wounds his eye, breaks out his tooth or even kills him, it is nothing—it is his money? On the contrary, he requires immediately the liberty of the aggrieved party or the death of the homicide.

Finally, the interest which servants inspired in Moses, shows itself in his desire to unite them directly to the family, and to have them participate in all the private and public rejoicings. At Rome masters took the place of slaves on the days of the Saturnalia ; it was a vain demonstration. Among the Hebrews, servants were seated as brothers by their sides. "Thou shalt make feasts of rejoicing, thou, thy son, thy daughter, thy man-servant, thy maid-servant, the stranger, the widow and the orphan."†

It is not necessary to go back to the servitude common among the shepherd patriarchs. Things could hardly be otherwise among little tribes that changed their residence each day, and whose chief resembled rather the absolute master of a great work-room than the governor of a plantation.

The prophets often rose up energetically against the violation of the laws with regard to servants. Under the government of Nehemiah a general assembly was convoked to remedy the abuses which had occasioned the captivity and the foreign occupation.‡

But after having spoken of the terms of domesticity among the Hebrews, how can we fail to recall the laws of the body of ancient nations concerning slaves,—in Crete, Sparta, Rome, Thessaly, Sicily? The history of Israel does not give a single instance of

* Ex. xxi. 21.   † Deut. xv. 11, 14.   ‡ Neh. v. ; Jer. xxx. 14

the insurrections which were common among these nations. As to modern and Christian nations, I come back to the assertion made at the head of this chapter ; it belongs not to them to censure either the Jews or the ancient republics. We know what servitudes their spiritual and temporal masters had imposed on these Jews vanquished by numbers, and deprived of their arms ; America and India are full of the remembrance of their exactions ; the affranchisement of the serfs dates only a few days back ; the slave trade still continues ; and even at this very hour in which I write (1827), in the face of a pretended Holy Alliance, extermination hovers over an entire population (Greece), which, reduced for ages to the state of slavery, only asks to awake under a new sun to break her chains.

———

The foregoing dissertation of Salvador sets at rest two points of the Mosaic law which the advocates of slavery have attempted to plead in their interest, viz., the tenure by which servants of a foreign race were held, and the extent of the Jubilee emancipation. In regard to the first, it is shown that the term "forever" is not absolute but relative ; it denotes the longer and often indefinite period until the Jubilee, in distinction from the fixed service of six years. One who should enter upon this larger term of service directly after a jubilee would hardly live out his forty or fifty years, and hence would serve "forever." It is admitted upon all sides, that every *Hebrew* servant went out free upon the day of Jubilee ; not excepting the servant who had sold his time indefinitely for debt, nor the servant who after the expiration of six years, had volunteered to remain with his master for an indefinite term. But of this last, whose ear was bored with an awl, it is said expressly that " he shall serve *forever.*" This term " forever," therefore, cannot be taken to mean absolute perpetuity. It covered the whole period, more or less, from the beginning of the contract until the subsequent Jubilee—"three years or the war." And Salvador's argument for the universality of the Jubilee, seems unanswerable.

But whatever interpretation is put upon these points, no warrant can be drawn from Moses for a perpetual chattel slavery; since the regulated domesticity of the Hebrew code, whatever its duration, had no one element or feature in common with chattelism. The so-called "buying" of a servant was a contract for a certain control over a person and his services, not the acquisition of a right of property in him as a thing. According to Philippson, "the deliverance of Israel from bondage being the foundation of their own national existence, the exclusion of slavery from among them was the prime condition of that existence. They must be a free people, a Nation of the Free."

The opening and closing remarks of Salvador must be ascribed to his Jewish prejudices against Christianity.

APPENDIX B.

THE following is an epitome of

EWALD'S VIEWS UPON HEBREW SERVITUDE.

As long as there are families more distinguished and wealthy than others, so long there will be persons of less note ready to attach themselves to the former; and in a patriarchal state of society, the more exclusive the position of a family, the closer will be the relation of these dependents, and the more likely are they to be regarded as property (eigenthum). Such appears to have been the most ancient form of slavery—in the patriarchal times.

We learn from the Old Testament some of the sources of slavery. The largest proportion of slaves were prisoners of war spared from the sword; but since among the Jews, this sparing of human booty was restricted, the number of male slaves in Israel could not be materially increased from this source. The ancient slave-trade may have sprung from the super-abundance of such prisoners, but kidnapping on a large scale appears to have originated in sudden hostile assaults which the Hebrew Prophets violently denounce, (Amos i. 6, 8) ; and manstealing is punished by the law as one of the greatest crimes. Indolence, poverty and moral depravity also led to slavery—many a one offering himself as a slave in order thereby to gain his living. Noah denounces slavery as the curse and consequence of moral degeneracy. (Gen. ix. 18–27.) After the patriarchal families came to live under an organized government, a debtor had to deliver up himself, his wife, and children, if he was unable to pay his debt. With the increase of the children of slaves, slavery expanded, especially in the more distinguished families, in which, moreover, the chief of the servants, the elder of the house, occupied a very prominent position. (Ex. xxi. 41, xxviii. 12 ; Gen. xiv. 14, xvii. 23–27.)

Slavery had thus become deeply rooted in the social state of the entire ancient world before the Hebrew law appeared. It could not be at once abolished ; but no religion of antiquity was so decidedly opposed to slavery as was this, from its peculiar origin, and its inextinguishable impulse,—none, at least, was so much opposed to all that is inhuman in slavery, or so surely prepared its abolition. The fundamental idea of the Hebrew religion explicitly declared this. Since Israel knew what the hardships of slavery were, they ought to treat their servants kindly, and as they themselves had complained of their sufferings in Egypt, and had rejoiced at their deliverance, they must, from this very circumstance, be unalterably opposed to slavery in any form. Their Law, therefore, rejected the traditional ideas of the position of slaves, and prescribed in their behalf, certain privileges to be enjoyed by the slave, be he a Hebrew or not.

1. In all the spiritual blessings of life he is to be on a par with the free. Before God they are equal and no distinction is, there-

fore, to be made in the enjoyment of the higher privileges of religion. They are to enjoy the Sabbath (Ex. xx. 11), and be circumcised (Gen. xvii. 10-14, 23-27, xxxiv. 22 ; Ex. xii. 44). They are to enter the congregation of the Lord like the free, and participate in the religious festivities (Ex. xii. 44, xii. 12-17, etc., xvi. 11-14). This was quite otherwise among heathen nations.

2. Civil rights are granted them as a protection against their masters, though in this respect not altogether equal to those of the free. Manslaughter is to be punished ; though the master is acquitted if the slave dies only after the lapse of several days ; if the slave is seriously injured he is free by law (Ex. xxi. 20, etc. 26, etc. comp. v. 52 ; also Job xxxi. 13-15). This of course applies to both male and female slaves.

In regard to a Hebrew slave, the law is, of course, still more lenient. He is to be liberated after six years, but has to leave behind him the wife given him by his master, and her children. (A seven years' service is a very ancient institution ; see Gen. xxix. 18. Lynch shows that such a custom still prevails in those regions.) Whoever does not wish to go free in the seventh year, has his ear bored, just as it is customary to pierce the nose of unruly animals (Cf. Z. xxxvii. 29 ; Ex. xxxviii. 4) and he then can remain forever. The service of a female Hebrew slave, for instance of a daughter sold by the father as a slave, was also limited to six years (Deut. xv. 12, 17) ; but the master was not permitted to sell her as a common slave (Ex. xxi. 7 ; Lev. xxv. 39-42). If he had taken her as a concubine, and thereby raised her to a higher position (for a concubine stood higher than a slave, somewhat like a *liberta*) he could not sell her to a stranger, but only *marry* her to a stranger. If he gave her to his son as a concubine, he was obliged to treat her like a daughter. If he kept her, and took another one besides her, he could not deprive her of anything after that, unless he let her go free (Ex. xxi. 7-11). If such a girl did not yet know her position, namely, if her master had not yet taken

6

her to himself nor given her as wife to a stranger, and somebody
slept with her, she could not be punished for adultery, but had to
bring a sin offering (Lev. xix. 20–22).

It appears that the liberation of a slave in the seventh year, must
have been soon after superseded by a law liberating him only in the
fiftieth year (Lev. xxv. 39–46).   It is true that in Deut. xv. 12–18,
the original law is reaffirmed with the addition that some assist-
ance be given to the liberated slave to maintain his independence ;
but even after the reformation, by King Josiah, this law could not
be carried into effect, as the relations of society had already become too intricate to admit of a return to the primitive simplicity.
It is noteworthy that in Lev. xxv. 40, it is recommended that a
Hebrew be treated like a hireling rather than like a slave, and an
attempt to abolish such slavery by law (without any permanent
success) was made under the last king of Judah (vol. iii., p. 744).
It appears to have been the common opinion, that a slave does
double the work of a hireling (Deut. xv. 18), which may have
interfered with the attempt ; the subsequent fall of the empire
rendered slavery impossible.   In the new Jerusalem slavery did
did not cease by law, but was confined to the few families of the
richest and most distinguished persons.

In the course of that period a new relation had sprung up, which
stands between slavery and free-labor, namely, *clientel.*   A client
is not the property of a master, he is far more independent ; but
binds himself to a family, and receives its protection in return for
certain services.   Such a client was still called in Israel a slave, but
was, in reality, something very different.   That such a relation
sprung up among the Hebrews in the passing away of the original
system of servitude, even as it existed among the ancient Arabs, is
shown on page 203.   The progress involved in this change, may
be inferred from the remarkable pictures of such a relation in the
Old Testament ; for whilst the ancient narrator represents the
sublime work of Moses as the servant of the Lord in the commun-

ity, under the figure of a superintendent, or the eldest of the slaves (Num. xii. 6–8), as described above, at a later period, the great Unnamed depicts the true nature of the future Messianic servant of the Jehovah as that of a *protégé* of the Lord, who executes his work independently. How much more appropriately can the working of a higher religion be represented under the latter figure. —*Die Alterthumer des Volkes Israel*, von Heinrich Ewald, Zweite Ausgabe, pp. 241–249.

The conclusion of Ewald, therefore, is equally strong with that of Salvador, that chattelism could have no place under the Mosaic code ; but that the servitude recognized and regulated by the Hebrew law, was based throughout upon certain economical and moral relations between men as men, and not upon the relation of a thing or an animal to its owner.

APPENDIX C.

ACTS OF COUNCILS IN BEHALF OF SLAVES.

By the seventh canon of the Council of Orange, A. D. 441, persons attempting to restrain the liberty of those whom the church had enfranchised or had received as *protégés*, were declared subject to condemnation. "In ecclesia manumissos, vel per testamentum ecclesiæ commendatos, si quis in servitutem, vel obsequium, vel ad colonariam conditionem imprimere tentaverit, animadversione ecclesiastica coerceatur."

The Council of Orleans, in 549, took decisive measures to protect the liberty of such as, in accordance with a laudable custom, had been manumitted in the churches, enjoining it upon the churches to defend the same. "Et quia plurimorum suggestione comperimus, eos qui in ecclesiis juxta patrioticam consuetudinem a servitiis fuerunt absoluti, pro libito quorumcumque iterum ad servitium revocari, impium esse tractavimus, ut quod in ecclesia Dei consideratione a vinculo servitutis absolvitur, irritum habeatur," etc.

The second Council of Macon, in 585, expressed its strong displeasure at the interference of the civil magistrates with the manumission authorized by the church, and enjoined it upon the bishops to take cognizance of such cases. "Indignum est enim, ut hi qui in sacrosancta ecclesia jure noscuntur legitimo manumissi, aut per epistolam, aut per testamentum, aut per longinquitatem temporis libertatis jura fruunter, a quolibet injustissime inquietentur. . . . . . Et quicumque a nobis de libertis latum decretum, superbiæ ausu prevaricare tentaverit, irreparabili damnationis suæ sententia feriatur."

The fourth Council of Toledo, in 633, assumed the defence both of the liberty and of the property of the freedmen committed to church patronage. "Liberti qui a quibuscumque manumissi sunt, atque ecclesiæ patrocinio commendati existunt, sicut regulæ antiquorum patrum constituerunt, sacerdotali defensione a cujuslibit insolentia protegantur ; sive in statu libertatis eorum, seu in peculio quod habere noscuntur." How beautiful an office for the Christian minister, to protect the freedman from insolence and wrong!

The curious reader will find collated in Balmes' Protestantism and Catholicity, a large number of decrees by various councils, authorizing the sale of the property of the church for the redemption of captives, denouncing man-stealing as a crime, and regulating the treatment of slaves by the dictates of justice and humanity. With much imperfection of method, and some serious exceptions in fact, the church of the middle ages was in spirit hostile to slavery, and devoted to its abolition.

In 1102, the Council of London pronounced the slave trade *infamous.* "Ne quis illud *nefarium negotium* quo hactenus in Anglia solebant homines sicut bruta animalia venundari, deinceps ullatenus facere præsumat."

APPENDIX D.

DUTY OF CHRISTIANS AT THIS CRISIS.

In the foregoing discussion I have confined myself to Biblical interpretations and historical testimony, as combining to show the anti-slavery spirit of the Bible. But I cannot dismiss these sheets without a word upon the present duty of Christian patriots in regard to slavery in these United States. I fear much from the prevailing disposition even of the known friends of the slave, to leave the system of slavery to the issue of the war. If the war shall be protracted until the Slave States are all held by the military forces of the government, and until a new order of society can be constructed under military protection, no doubt slavery will be exterminated by the war. But if the war shall stop short of this, or if Congress shall repeal the Confiscation Act and other laws that have favored emancipation, it will be found that the liberation of tens of thousands of slaves is not the abolition of slavery.

If Louisiana or Georgia should speedily return to their loyalty to the Union, what shall hinder the revival of their slave code, even against those whom the Proclamation of January 1st, 1863, declared free, but who have not escaped from the hand of their masters? And the President's theory of guaranteeing to each loyal State the integrity of its local institutions, might place him in the false position of rebuilding that which his proclamation sought to destroy. At all events there must be a collision of courts and of powers, if not of arms, growing out of such complications.

From the very commencement of the war, it has seemed to me that each seceded State, by the act of secession, had vacated its organic existence, and that all State laws and institutions had ceased to be, throughout the area of the rebellion, which now reverts to the government of the United States to be administered by territorial laws. Thus it is made impossible for slavery to exist again after the war : being prohibited in the territories of the United States, it would never be instituted in the States to be . hereafter erected out of those territories, and it must speedily die in the border States.

But this is not the theory of the administration in the conduct of the war ; and, therefore, considering the uncertainties of war, it behooves all Christian patriots to labor directly and earnestly for the overthrow of slavery through the facilities which the war opens for that end. If the sagacious recommendation of the President in his last annual message—bating the length of time for its consummation—could be urged through Congress and the State legislatures, ratifying the liberty of all persons made free in the course of the war, and decreeing abolition with compensation, as a measure of the organic national law, all danger of the reorganization of slavery and of the slave power after the war, would be effectually removed. There is here a great work for Christian sentiment and action, and we must take heed, lest in waiting for events, we lose our opportunity.